WYSIWYG Christianity

Young People and Faith in the 21st century

by

Trevor Stubbs

The Listening People

For many helpful young people of England and France

without whom this book could not have been written.

First published in 2005 by
The Listening People
84 South Street
Bridport, Dorset
DT6 3NW
United Kingdom

Scripture quotations from the
New Revised Standard Version ©

ISBN – 0-9550100-0-4

Printed by Creeds the Printers, Broadoak, Bridport, Dorset DT6 5NL
01308 423411

Contents

ACKNOWLEDGEMENTS

This book has grown out of many years of working with young people as a priest in the Church of England. I wish to record my thanks to those who have put up with my ministry in those years – those who have been experimented upon and those who never got the attention they deserved. I am most grateful for the huge generosity that people have shown me, especially in the months that it took to write this book. In the Spring of 2004 young folk from the length and breadth of England, and many parts of France too, have been extremely helpful in talking frankly and openly about themselves and their feelings. This is not easy for young people who are naturally nervous of the judgements that their peers and older generations may make. I have met some pretty brave young people and teenagers and I want to thank them.

I am also grateful to the many youth workers, members of the clergy and older people in society in general who have given me time and opportunities, as well as contributing their ideas. I wish to thank my area bishop, Bishop Tim Thornton, the Bishop of Sherborne, who has given me constant encouragement throughout the project and written the foreword. My colleagues in the Bridport Team have been helpful and very patient, as have the people of the parish in not only allowing me to take a three months' sabbatical, but taking a real interest in the project.

Finally I must thank my family, my three sons for helping me to understand on more than a few things, and my wife Tina who has advised and accompanied me throughout, and without whom this book would never have been written.

Trevor Stubbs
Bridport

February 2005

FOREWORD

It is a truism to state that we live in an age in which young people do not flock to churches of any variety. It is also true to say that young people are as interested in matters of spirituality and questions relating to who they are and ideas of meaning as any other generation, indeed probably more so. Trevor Stubbs in this book researches the ways in which young people are still interested in matters of 'God' and the questions they are asking, as well as looking at the church and churches and the ways in which they are not connecting with young people today.

There is a mismatch, a breakdown in communication and it is serious. I was talking recently to some 15 year old art students and showing them what a bishop wears in church, and talking about my illustrious predecessor Aldhelm (first bishop of Sherborne in the year 705 AD). When I was fully robed and mitred, I stood in front of them and one young lad shook his head and said, "That is a fashion disaster!"

This book is therefore timely and important, not only because it helpfully analyses the problem, but also because it contains much wisdom from a long and distinguished career as a parish priest. Here there are practical suggestions and ideas for reconnecting with young people.

Trevor is a passionate priest who cares for all people. He has found a special heart for young people, and his claim that the Christian story is one that has much to offer them is a heart felt one. As Trevor points out so well in this book, it is when the church becomes too much an organization, and an inward looking and speaking one, that it fails all people, but especially fails young people.

The church needs to maintain the right confidence it can, and should have, in Jesus Christ and recognize that, as Jesus and his first disciples, we need to communicate, to build relationships and to be honest one with another. All of those are qualities and ways of relating which young people understand. I hope by reading this book you will be heartened and find ways to carry on engaging and relating not only to young people but find ways to be real, to tell it as it is, with people of all ages.

The Rt. Revd Tim Thornton
Bishop of Sherborne

February 2005

1. Introduction

"I just can't understand young people these days", proclaimed an old lady celebrating her ninetieth birthday as she scrutinized her grandchildren and their 'kids' (as she called them), "I just don't know what has got into them! Why, when we were young we knew what we could and couldn't do, and we were happy with it."

Allowing for the inevitable failure of the mind to remember exactly what the world was like more than eighty years before, and our tendency to forget the bad, this old person is recognizing an important truth. The culture the young enjoy is very different from that in which she grew up. It isn't just about the visible things like aeroplanes, televisions, DVDs, computers and mobile telephones, it is about the way we think about the world – our basic cultural assumptions. What should life really be about? What are we aiming for? What do we mean by success, and how do we measure it? How do we define right and wrong, and who says? Where does God (or the beyond) fit into all this, and what about organised religion? How do religion, God, spirituality and society connect today? Over the past forty years children have been taught to think critically as well as absorb, to marshal knowledge and to find out things for themselves (using libraries, encyclopaedias and now the Internet). Vocational training is increasingly college based rather than learning 'on the job' at work. This is a world away from the "three Rs" up to age 14, followed by jobs or apprenticeships for most of the population. The pressures of world communications leave youngsters open to exploitation, temptation and opportunities unimagined 50 years ago. But the hardship and the suffering of war have had a great impact on the lives of those who were young in the 1930s and 1940s – experiences quite unknown by most of their grandchildren.

It is no wonder that different generations find it hard to keep in touch with each other. It is understandable that some have given up trying. They read different publications, listen to different radio programmes and increasingly live in different parts of the country. Yet both young and old are conscious of this break and often feel deprived. No generation wants to be excluded or condemned, and all suffer if contact is lost. The old have an incredible amount to contribute to the current world, but feel out of their depth. The young sometimes feel judged and misunderstood. The churches find themselves trying to relate to varying cultures, with all their fears and suspicions, and are often perceived as failing. And yet Christianity, I believe, can have a great impact on our world and its future. If there is truly a God who loves the world so much that he is willing to live and die in it (John 3:16) then we have Good News to share that has both power and eternal purpose. As a member of the Church (and more especially the Kingdom of God), I am excited by the thought. But how are we going to embark on this venture of sharing the message of Jesus Christ across the barriers of age and culture?

For two millennia, beginning with the Roman Empire, Europe has been a home of Christianity. From here, as nations have explored the globe looking for all that might make them materially rich, they have also taken the Christian Gospel. So today throughout these former colonies, there are well established indigenous churches, branches of the old European denominations. In many of these countries, including the United States of America, the churches can claim large proportions of the population where young people form a vibrant sector of the membership. In Western Europe, however, the churches, especially the old traditional mainstream denominations, have been in decline for half a century – a decline that shows no sign of abating.

The purpose of this book is to explore some of the reasons for this trend in western Europe, and to suggest ways of addressing the problem. To call this a problem is to reveal my own stance on the question. I write from the standpoint of a parish priest who has worked for the past thirty years in Yorkshire (including in an urban priority area), in rural Australia and now in a coastal town in the south of England. I am not concerned to write a social survey from a detached point of view. I come with a conviction that the way of Christ is indeed "Good News", and that people who have not heard it are missing out. My purpose is to do some practical theology that may point to some pragmatic steps to reverse the drift.

Some take the view that trends such as these are beyond our control, all we can do is tinker at the margins. Would it not be better to accept things as they are and see what turns up? Living in a small town beside the sea I know the power of the tides and the currents and the risks involved for those who attempt to swim against them. We seem to be, through all the modern means of communication, at the mercy of forces from outside, which, at first sight, rarely mention God. Even where there is a genuine effort to share faith, local churches can appear homespun and amateur in comparison, and lack impact. American style media Christianity has not caught on in Europe – perhaps its appeal is too broad-brush, too loud, even for youthful Europeans, sensitive to centuries of refining history. But there are examples of European revival that are impacting on young people, some larger than others. Some of these I was able to find in a short sabbatical tour of England and France in the Spring of 2004.

But it is almost universally true in Western Europe that it is the young people who are not identifying with the mainstream churches. As the congregations age, so the generation gap increases, and churches come across to young people as not only amateur, but outmoded. In my part of the world many older people seem to have reconciled themselves to this, and even, in some cases, relaxed into accepting the situation with a little relief because young people bring change, and change is something they would rather not cope with. There is, sadly, among some, a short-term view that says that the churches will still be around for the next few years, long enough to see them into the next world, so why not let things be. It is not that most older people do not want to see young church members, but they expect them to accept the traditional cultures of worship and lifestyles along with faith. In any case, ageing congregations with ageing priests and ministers to lead them frequently do not know where to begin to address the question of evangelizing the young. They are unable to enter the cultures that prevail among the younger generations, and even where they do, lack the ability, contacts, energy, time or imagination to attract teens and twenties. Active people in churches with ageing populations are often caught up in caring for one another. Ministering to those who are ill, lonely, bereaved, housebound (or enabling and caring for others to do so) takes up most of the time of the parish clergy and hard working lay people. Yet, if we truly believe that the Gospel is indeed good news, then it is good news for everyone. Jesus Christ has changed the lives of countless people for over two millennia in Europe and seeks to continue to do so, whatever their generation.

The Church is proving to be very popular in the third world, particularly in Africa where there is so much suffering. The Anglican Mothers' Union, for example, founded in the age of growing social concern in the second half of the nineteenth century in England to promote family values and to support women in adversity, is hardly known among young people in England where a large section of its membership consists of middle aged and older women, but it is of significant importance to the women of Africa beset by poverty, AIDS and the effects of war and famine.[1] Here Christianity ministers to the needs for community, peace, love and hope. But this longing is not confined to the third world. Older people in Western Europe sometimes assume that young people have no interest in God. Brought up in a world where religion and science were at war with each other, a world in which consumerism often prevailed, senior generations are often unaware of the huge interest and longing among young people for something more than material goods, intellectual achievement and security. There is a growing thirst among young people of Europe for a sense of meaning, a search for 'spirituality'. In Britain, there is a growing interest in the study of the philosophy of religion in schools, where there has been a greater take up in GCSE and A level Religious Studies courses.[2] Universities that offer Religious Studies or Theology are not experiencing recruiting difficulties for these subjects. Younger generations are also exploring New Age religion, or turning to more intense fundamentalist approaches to faith. Even the use of drugs is demonstrating a dissatisfaction with the quality of life from an inner point of view – rich young people as well as poorer ones are attracted by the promise of an escape into an "inner"something. But there is no short cut to the discovery that there is something, some One, *out there,* beyond the mind, that provides ultimate meaning to life, in whom we can find an inner peace.

If young people are searching, then the tide is not against those who seek to share the good news. We are not attempting the impossible if what we are about is honestly announcing the Kingdom of God. We are, however, having to accept that the ways in which we have chosen to express that good news in Western Europe over the past century and a half will no longer impact on the young.

The Gospel has become lost because "church culture" is strange and confusing to young postmodern minds learning to live in a "fluid" society – a place where nothing is dependable and solid as it once seemed. Trust does not come easily and will not be accorded to anything that seems to be located anywhere other than where it claims to be. The church must reflect the Gospel it proclaims or else it will not be seen as "WYSIWYG". This new word, an acronym meaning "what you see is what you get", comes to us from the world of computing and sums up the importance of being down to earth and uncomplicated. It means that what you see on a VDU screen which exists "virtually" will be reproduced faithfully when printed out as hard copy (i.e. on paper in the "real" world). The message must "check out" if it is to be believed, and the trouble is that in many cases the Gospel and church's witness do not co-incide, when looked at through through the eyes of 21st century young people.

For some, the old cultures have become so embedded in their life of faith that they have become part and parcel of it. Older generations find it hard to distinguish between, on the one hand, what is the culture of their own particular European tradition and, on the other, what pertains to the Kingdom of God. These religious cultural accretions are frequently intertwined with other cultures that express themselves in music, dress, relationships and mores that young people find alien. Nevertheless, the Church has the "keys of the Kingdom of God" (Matt 16:19), and the responsibility to hand on faith (Matt 28:19-20). If we accept that responsibility – and it is difficult to see how Christians can be faithful to the teachings of Christ without sharing the Good News of God's love for everyone of no matter what age, culture, or background – then we have to discover meaningful ways of fulfilling it. Danièle Hervieu-Léger[3], a French social scientist, has pointed clearly to a "chain of memory" whereby traditions of faith are passed on down the generations. She suggests that unless things change the "memory" of what it means to be a Christian, an understanding of the Scriptures and Christian religious tradition (not just the recent cultural accretions but tradition extending back to the beginning of Christianity) will be lost. Grace Davie[4] has identified the same processes in her extensive surveys of the churches in Europe. The people of God can no longer rely on schools to preserve this chain of memory. In France since the Revolution the laws of *laicité* have insisted on religion being taught wholly as a secular fact of history and society[5]. The effect of this is that, unless brought to church, or sent to church schools (for which they have to pay), young people have little understanding of the possibility of spiritual fulfilment for themselves in Christianity. The result has been an increasing decline in the impact of Christianity on the nation and on the numbers of people worshipping. This is being experienced even in Brittany which has up till now escaped the greatest impact of the secular culture. In England, although religion has always been part of the curriculum, the same is true. In most schools, religion is taught from a historical angle and is inclusive of all major world religions.[6] Outside of church schools (and indeed in many of these too), children are aware of only a few bible stories. Detailed knowledge of the bible and Christian doctrine is missing. If our young people are to obtain an opportunity to explore the spiritual depths of the Christian faith, they will have to receive it from the Church. The Church, therefore, is obliged to tackle the question of passing on the Good News to the young, and with some urgency.

Before I attempt to suggest ways this might be done, we need to look more closely at what makes it so hard for people to communicate across the generations. We live in a fast changing world, and we have different strategies of coping with it. Chapters two and three examine the way the speed of change in society has increased and what the postmodern culture is all about. This section is included to set the ideas of the later chapters in their proper context, but you might like – in true postmodern style – to skip these and come back to them later. In chapter four we reflect on the particular situation for young people in today's world. Chapter five explores what the Bible and Christian traditions have to say that is especially relevant today, and in chapter six we will look at the particular problems the people of God are facing that prevent them from being WYSIWYG. In the final section I address the challenge of what the Church must do to re-invent itself, and suggest some practical approaches to enable it to fulfil its tasks of mission and ministry. Let us, then, begin by delving into the cultures of our world and explore what it is that separates young from old so profoundly.

2. A Fast Changing World

For those who live in parts of the world within "Western" cultures, the concept of a world in flux is axiomatic. The way of life that their grandparents, and even parents, pursued is often vastly different from what pertains today. Although we may agree on the fact of change, there is disagreement on the rate of that change. I contend that our worldview in Europe is changing faster than it has ever done before. Things have always changed, but the last fifty years have seen an unprecedented revision of expectation and culture. This needs to be fully appreciated and accepted if we are to understand how young and old interact today. The increased rate of change is so steep that much of the time younger generations make cultural assumptions sometimes unrecognized, and certainly not shared, by older generations. If we add to this the growth in life expectancy, then the distance between teenagers and the oldest people, many of whom are still actively involved in things, is enormous. Among some of the older people, but by no means all, there is a resistance to some of this change.

The church has always proved a bastion of historical tradition and people look to it to preserve the past – yet among its membership there are those who embrace the changing culture with enthusiasm. Christians have been among the instigators of change as well among the resistance. Alongside the protagonists there have been those from the Christian community who have played an important role in providing the spiritual and moral heart of European society. The Church has had to accept change, and where it has moved with the times it has enabled society to reflect the Christian principles of love, forgiveness, reconciliation and hope. Although a few would want to question it, most people believe that we live in a better world today than in the past. Nostalgia can deceive us, but the lessons of the twentieth century have, to some extent, still to be learned. Born in 1948, I am fortunate enough to belong to the first generation never to have seen a major European war, for example. Some of this may have been due to the fear of a nuclear holocaust, but by no means all of it. Life, today, despite its pressures is better than it was for many communities in Europe, and our moral sense of justice is more developed. Whilst we no longer live in "Christendom", in one sense the world is a more "Christian" place. This has come about through the continual witness of the Christian community to what they believe God wants for his creation – the values of the Kingdom of God as set out in the New Testament.[7]

Let us turn our attention to the way things have changed over the past few centuries. It is important to realize that change is not a novel experience, something that has only occurred in our own life times, even if the rate of change has increased. It is also important to note that change has always been resisted but never overcome.

Communication is the Key to the Speed of Change

Between the Norman conquest (1066) and the fourteenth century the way of life lived by most Europeans, both rich and poor, changed relatively little from generation to generation. Most of the scholarship was religious in nature since those with the time and opportunity for it were monks. Books were hand written, mostly in Latin, and were kept in the libraries of the religious houses. But the introduction of the printing press in the mid fifteenth century changed all that.[8] The speed of change depends on the speed and effectiveness of human communication. As books became increasingly available, so more and more people were able to contribute their thoughts on the world and their own condition. By the end of the fifteenth and the beginning of the sixteenth centuries, technology was so improved that revolutionary theories (like those of Copernicus (1473-1543) and others) about the nature of the Earth and the Heavens could be put to the test. Improved ship design enabled explorers to confirm[9] the spherical shape of our planet, and the Ptolemaic theory of the structure of the universe began to be questioned.

Easier communication in scientific circles had great religious implications. The more that scholars understood about the workings of the universe, the less they needed to recourse to God as an explanation for the details of how things worked. One of the greatest scholars of the period, Leonardo da Vinci (1452-1519), made such progress that some of his work, especially in the field of anatomy, was discouraged by a threatened church hierarchy. Thinking about God became more informed as more people had access to the Bible, and began to be dissatisfied with the way the Church reflected what they read in the Scriptures. Reformers sprang up and the Bible was being translated into vulgar tongues. More people, albeit still the privileged few, were being given a choice in the way they responded to the ultimate questions of life. Martin Luther, disturbed by the exploitation of the people by the Church in Rome, published his ninety-five theses in Wittenberg in 1517. A new surge of change was under way, and the degree of choice in religion further increased. The speed of change was accelerating.

Church and Politics

The sixteenth century Reformation was, of course, more than a religious event. Before that time Church and State in Europe were so intertwined that politics and faith were almost one piece. The motivations of the German princes in promoting Luther's challenge of the Pope were bound up with the politics of power. In England, Henry VIII (1491 – 1547) was not attracted to the theology of Protestantism at all, but the opportunity to seize the initiative from the Pope, and to take over the wealth of the church was irresistible. The Church was governed by princes, and in turn, temporal politics were infiltrated by religious reformers.

It was assumed that everyone in Europe who was not a Jew or an immigrant "infidel", was automatically a Christian of some kind. But the Reformation produced an age of choice in religion. Certainly the politics of the region played a huge part in determining that choice – but for the thinker there was a debate to be entered into. Instead of absolute and given Faith to be simply accepted, the search for truth was becoming a dialogue. Of course most of the protagonists in the debate were uncompromising and the debate was almost always confrontational (even between the various Protestant factions – so much power was at stake) but the doors were open for theological inquiry in a way they had never been before. Scripture was being translated into the languages of the people. Henry VIII was not slow in perceiving the dangers of this to his continued control of both Church and realm. William Tyndale, translator of the bible into English, was in permanent conflict with him until Tyndale's execution in Brussels in 1536.

With the diminution of papal power an age of theological debate had come about, a debate that was eventually to move people away from believing they had absolute truth, into travelling a road of discovery of truth; from acceptance to exploration.

Increased knowledge stimulated yet further change, and also the conservative opposition that accompanied it. The Church in Rome, through the counter Reformation centred on the council of Trent (1545-1563), sought to reinforce its power base by reaffirming absolutes of faith and practice. Yet, at the same time, the academic world was moving resolutely towards the period we now know as the Enlightenment.

The Enlightenment

Science and mathematics were leaping forward – especially in the lands outside papal control. Nevertheless even in Italy, despite the suppression of the printed word where it was deemed necessary (the Index of Forbidden Books was introduced in 1559[10]), it was impossible to prevent this increase in knowledge. In the following century, the seventeenth, Galileo exhibited the first telescope on record in 1609, studied the moon and the planets and, through observation and mathematical deduction, came to the conclusion that the Copernican picture of the solar system, in which the Sun was in the centre rather than the Earth, was the correct view. Copernicus works were put on the *Index* and Galileo, despite remaining a faithful Catholic, found himself in serious trouble for the rest of his life. He was faced with a choice – to accept the conclusions of his science (which he did not believe contravened faith in God) or renounce them and accept the views of the Church. Galileo's *Dialogue on the Two Chief World Systems* (1630) is a classic expression of the dilemma faced by scientists and scholars in Catholic circles.[11] A rift between men of learning and the church teaching on the issue of "truth" was widening at every new discovery.

René Descartes (1596-1650) emphasized the importance of scepticism in thinking. Nothing should be taken on trust – the only thing of which he could be absolutely sure was his own existence ("I think, therefore I am").[12] Sir Isaac Newton (1642-1727) was a most celebrated physicist in his day. Although he was deeply religious and perceived the hand of God in nature, he felt the Christian Church had lost its way in the fourth century when it defined the nature of Christ.[13] Other scholars of the Enlightenment in the century and a half that followed did not have the same concern for either Christianity or God. Deism[14] was popular in England and Ireland among scholars such as Edward Herbert (d. 1648) and John Toland (d. 1722), and also, in France, through the influence of Voltaire (1694-1788). Deism, although it held to the existence of God, denied the validity of revelation or the teaching of the Church. This was followed, especially in France, by the atheism and materialism of many of the later *philosophes* of the late 18th century, such as Denis Diderot (1713-1784).

In the Enlightenment scholars were co-operating across Europe, ignoring political boundaries wherever they could.[15] Inventions and discoveries were changing the world outside of the control of prelates, princes and armies. Nevertheless ordinary people still relied on the States for their security, or lack of it. Religious opinions were often the cause of unrest. In England where, despite the absence of the Pope in politics, the disputes among "high church" and Puritan had been at the root of the struggles between Parliament and King that led to the English Civil War (1642-1649). With the failure of the "Commonwealth" a more tolerant climate had emerged. Neither Parliament nor King had absolute power, and the Church, so long as Rome was kept at bay, concerned itself less with national politics in favour of a constitutional position.

In France, however, intimate links between monarch and church persisted until the end of the 18th century. The autocratic rule of Louis XIV, the "Sun King", (1643-1715) and his successors came to an abrupt end in the French Revolution. Both regime and church became increasingly unpopular among the general populace. For example, it is said that the villages around the abbey of Cluny in Saône-et-Loire were so turned off by the exploitation of the region and its people by the monks that even in the middle of the twentieth century the local people were still suspicious of monastic religion. The Taizé Community report that some of the local people were, in the beginning, dubious about the founding of their order. With the ending of the monarchy in France in 1793, the power of the Church was lost. Napoleon "nationalised" the church in order to limit its power and ensure it did nothing to overturn the Revolution. The *Concordat* of 1801 introduced the idea of a secular government under which institutions of faith live separate but regulated lives. This was to become known in France as *laicité*, which persists to this day. The *Concordat* recognised Catholics, Protestants and Jews. (Today there are moves to include Islamic institutions within its framework, but so far this has not happened. The recent clashes over the freedom of Muslim girls to wear the "veil" at school stems largely from the concern that such religious expression contravenes the spirit of *laicité*). The importance of the French Revolution to the political scene across Europe cannot be underestimated. Although the threat of Napoleon united the surrounding lands and served to focus the minds of ordinary people away from class war for a time, the upper classes understood their vulnerability and were on the whole more conducive to change. The middle classes were more conscious of their power should they wish to use it.

In England the rise of Methodism was a focus for the working people, but it was based around religious revival and although it called for social change, did not call for changes in social order. So long as the squire and the "county set" allowed their servants and workers to attend Methodists revival meetings and worship, the system was largely unquestioned. What was happening was that when it came to religion the people in Britain were permitted a choice. The adherents of the established Church may not have liked it, but they allowed it. From the beginning of the 19th century non-conformist churches were springing up around the country – especially in rural areas where many villages boasted a choice of places of worship. The culture of choice in religion was now permeating to the lower classes. More people were able to read and write and better communication meant greater diversity. The novel, which often reflected on moral choices made by their characters, was growing in popularity. Authors such as Daniel Defoe (c. 1660-1731), Henry Fielding (1707-1754), Laurence Sterne (1713-1768), William Godwin (1756-1836), Jane Austen (1775-1817) and others less well known were widely read by the literate. Within the stories people were reading were criticisms of contemporary society, and it was becoming increasingly possible for less privileged people to have an informed opinion about things.

The Industrial Revolution

The eighteenth and nineteenth century Industrial Revolution[16] is probably the greatest social upheaval of recent history. The population of Britain and the West in general moved from an agrarian society based around agriculture with its seasons and village life, to an urban world of factories churning out their products (and their unsavoury polluting by-products) summer and winter alike. Many workers lost both self-identity and self respect. Callum Brown traces the decline of Christianity in Britain to this time:

> Religious decline in Britain is intellectually located in the distance between two 'worlds', the pre-industrial and the industrial. Pre-industrial society was the world we have lost – a world of innocence,

> humble spirituality, economic simplicity and social harmony. Industrialization and the growth of large cities started the rapid decline of the churches, religious belief and religious morality. Piety and machines were disconnected and opposing. By contrast, the world we have found was and remains a world of technology, competitiveness, and social dislocation, with piety a transient signifier of class identity. (Brown, 16)

The new society threw up its champions. The bleakness and sheer exploitation of the mill workers and their families pricked the conscience of the nation. Churchmen were not immune to the needs, and many men and women dedicated themselves to addressing both the political and social needs at national, local and individual levels. But, although ordinary people came to be cared for *by* the church, they often ceased to be part of it. The conditions that gave rise to the late twentieth century calls of Liberation Theology in South America[17] and elsewhere for the church to be "of" the poor rather than "for" the poor could be seen in this period in Britain.[18] Church membership was identified with the upper classes. With the best of motives some of the mill owners built their workers churches and Sunday schools to ensure their souls were properly cared for. In Heckmondwike, near Dewsbury, West Yorkshire the Upper Chapel, a Congregationalist foundation was erected for the people who worked at the nearby woollen mill. It was so large it became known as the "Cathedral of the North" and when it was first built was full every Sunday. But workers had no choice about attending – their pay was docked if they were not there, or they failed to send their children to the Sunday school. By the middle of the century there were three Congregationalist and two Methodist chapels in Heckmondwike all associated with the "gaffers" of local factories in the town.

It is not surprising that socialism, as it challenged the capitalism of the Industrial Revolution, was to identify the Church with capitalism and why Karl Marx so famously called it the "opium of the people". The church, for its part, roundly rejected socialism – even the very gentle sort of Robert Owen (the father of English Socialism)[19] himself a mill-owner. Where the working folk were being encouraged to speak up for themselves they often found themselves in conflict with religion.

In many ways the working man had ceased to have a heart for religion. The women, however, were different. "it was their attachment to domesticity and all the virtues located with that, which sustained discursive Christianity in the age of modernity," claims Brown (Brown, 195). Vestiges of this were to last into the 1960s until women were no longer to be found predominantly in the kitchen and laundry.

The Impact of Darwinism

The idea that God might not exist had not, until the middle of the nineteenth century, troubled many beyond the studies of the learned. Among the rank and file of ordinary men and women, God was seen as creator of the wonders of heaven and earth. But gradually these wonders were being explained by science, and the boundaries of what seemed to be miraculous were pushed back. With the publication of Darwin's *Origin of the Species* in 1859 the debate reached thousands. The freedom to question the tenets of religion had increased to a disturbing level. A few negative views by academic minds might be tolerated, but the *Origin of the Species* became an instant best seller! Its first edition of 1,250 copies sold on the day of publication and hundreds of thousands of copies of subsequent editions were sold in the following few years. More and more children were being taught to read in Western Europe and America, and more and more of them wanted to read Darwin and his contemporaries.

The Church perceived that not only the institution of the Church was under threat (which was frightening enough) but now the very existence of God was being called into question. English churchmen sought to debunk the new thinking. In 1860 Bishop Samuel Wilberforce engaged Thomas Huxley, a biologist and proponent of Darwinism, in a debate that did not do justice to the integrity of those who continued to claim Christ as their Saviour. Although there were those who had open minds on the subject, and whose faith was not undermined by an acceptance of evolution, there was a felt need to reaffirm the certainties of the supernatural. "There was", says Gabriel Hebert, "a denial of the miraculous on account of the uniformity of nature and the universal validity of the laws of nature" (Hebert, 21). Wilberforce (known as "Slippery Sam" because of his debating technique) demanded of Huxley on which side of his family he claimed to be descended from an ape? The scientific historian James Moore says of Huxley that, "warfare was his favourite metaphor by which to describe the scientific pursuit of truth in the face of ecclesiastical constraints on truth seeking and failures in truth telling." (Moore, 58). He replied that he would rather have an ape as a ancestor than someone like Wilberforce who "misused his talents to attack a theory he did not understand" (Bowler, 184).

Some philosophers and writers were caught up in thinking through what a post-Christian world, a world without God, would be like. George Eliot, for example, is concerned that values should be maintained. Believing God was, for her, "inconceivable", immorality "unbelievable", but duty nonetheless "peremptory and absolute" (Himmelfarb, 27). Others used their skill to promote their religious convictions. Universities were divided in their response to the changes. Conservative by nature, some were reluctant to allow free rein for their professors. In 1853 F. D. Maurice published his book, *Theological Essays* which shocked the principal of King's College, London where he was professor. The college council decided Maurice's "doctrines were dangerous" and he was asked to resign.[20] Others, were encouraging their theologians to use the new thinking to analyse faith, religion and the scriptures in a scientific way. Maurice was subsequently elected to become professor of moral philosophy at Cambridge in 1866. This was an age of choice in religion as had never before been experienced. Religion and science were in debate, but a debate that was no longer in the control of religious or state authorities. The graph of the speed of change was becoming relentlessly steeper. Not only the bourgeois and the learned, but the mass of the people were deeply effected.

The Industrial Revolution of the 19th century had led to huge demographic changes as people moved from the countryside to the towns. The new machines displaced workers in one area and led to their exploitation in others. Conscientious middle class Christians of different denominations were becoming socially conscious. The second half of the 19th century saw the rise of General Booth's Salvation Army, Robert Raikes' Sunday Schools (designed to teach working class children the three 'Rs' as well as religion), Mary Sumner's Mothers' Union (in which middle class women were pledging themselves to social action), William Carlyle's Church Army to help the poorest on the streets of London, the Church of England "Waifs and Strays" Society (later to become known as the Children's Society), foreign missionary societies, and countless other voluntary, social and philanthropic organizations.

As well as the Christian, atheistic social philosophy was also on the move. Marks and Engels' communist ideologies were gaining popularity. Religion for them was a means of control of the masses which anaesthetized the people to their condition, and was to be opposed. This kind of social theory challenged the very core of the social structure that had sustained society for millennia.

The Emergence of a New Youth Sub-Culture

In this period people began to realize that young people were making a separate contribution to popular culture. Christopher Livesey comments that, "the idea of youth as a distinct phase in social development is itself a relatively modern phenomenon – one that is characteristic of advanced industrial societies with well-developed educational systems."[21] In these passionate decades we see the beginnings of the feminist movement and, in a different way (for they were not the same) the "new women" who, in theory at least, rejected marriage because they wished to challenge the division of life into two spheres, work and home, to which women were confined to the latter (Himmelfarb,189). These young women shocked the late Victorian scene, as did the liberated men of the *fin de siècle* movement of which Oscar Wilde was the epitome. They were, of course, a limited few. Most people needed to be "respectable" to ensure they earned a living, especially the working classes, but whether or not they were free to choose them, alternative life-styles were out there and available to be dreamed of and read about in their publications, novels and plays. Communication is the key to questioning and debating, and thus to choice. Here again we see that the more communication is possible, as more and more young people are able to read, the greater the tendency to explore, question and experiment.

In the early 1900s most people were, in economic terms, more prosperous on the whole than they had been fifty years earlier. Ordinary people were becoming mobile, even in the remoter countryside where only the better off could afford a horse, because the bicycle made it possible to get about in ways they had not been able to do before. In rural areas the choice of a bride had been limited by the distance a man could walk to find one. With access to a safety bicycle he could visit villages ten times the distance. It is held locally that, in the late 19th century, the bicycle revolutionised rural Dorset as much as any other single change in society.

The Emergence of Biblical Criticism

Within Christianity, faith and Scripture were questioned and investigated in a manner heretofore unimaginable. Biblical scholars such as Alfred Loisy(1857-1940), Baron Friedrich von Hügel (1852-1925), David Strauss (1808-1874), and others were changing the theological scene. Charles Gore (1853-1922), editor of the celebrated collection of essays entitled *Lux Mundi: A Series of Studies in the Religion of the Incarnation* in 1889, in which progressive Christian scholarship was promoted, was a champion of this liberal Christian thinking which led to the religious Modernist movement in the first decade of the 20th century. This movement encouraged the debate about truth and, following the concepts of social evolution (that grew from the Lamarkian and Darwinian theories of Evolution in the natural world [22]), promoted the idea of a progressive religious awareness and knowledge. The "pilgrimage" model of understanding faith was becoming popular as scholars exposed the Bible to literary and historic criticism with astonishing results. A new enthusiasm for the things of God was emerging, not based on tradition or authority, but on discovering truth.

All this was indicative of unprecedented change, the velocity of which for some, especially those with social and religious power who had the most to loose, was alarming. It seemed as if it was no longer possible in an age of such new thinking, and social and economic flux, for anyone to impose belief on people again. But just as the Reformation produced a Counter Reformation that took the Church further along conservative lines, so this period of challenge had an equal counter assault.

Reactions within Established Religion at the End of the 19th Century

The reaction to this new freedom from both Catholic and Protestant churches was to become even more closed and authoritarian. In Rome, despite being beset from the invasion of the French, the Catholic Church persisted with the First Vatican Council (1869-1870) under Pius IX. The effective element of this council was to bestow even more power, of a religious nature, on the Pope. As his temporal power decreased, his ecclesiastical power became greater. In 1870 the Council passed the doctrine of Papal Infallibility. Subsequent Popes were to become increasingly conservative. In 1907 Pius X launched an all out assault on Modernism introducing his own form of Catholic fundamentalism, "*intégrisme*", which removed all element of choice for Catholics. Obedience to *the* Faith required unquestioned obedience to the Church, and the Church was immutable – there was to be no experimentation permitted for Catholic scholars.

A similar reaction was happening in Protestant circles, especially in America, which was having an impact on Evangelical churches in Europe. Scholars such as Charles Hodge (1797-1878) and Benjamin Warfield (1851-1921) were troubled by the subjection of the Bible to literary criticism and were promoting a view that it should be regarded as the inspired Word of God and understood literally without further questioning. Scripture was unquestionable and should not be subject to debate. This was the beginning of what was later to become known as "fundamentalism". At the same time as Pius X was attacking the Modernists, Protestants in America published a series of twelve books called *The Fundamentals* beginning in 1909. By the time the twelfth book was published three million copies had been sold. The ordinary person was caught up in a battle for his or her soul. These movements reached down to local congregations, and meetings and missions were held for the common people to attend. People were told that there was only one way to choose if they wanted eternal salvation – but unlike some of their forefathers, they had to make that choice consciously.

People Power

The battles of the early 20th century were not limited to words. The First World War threw into full view the changes in technology and communication and revealed that it was no longer possible for the upper classes of Europe to fall out without involving the whole population. Within a few years, the masses had their say in Russia, women won the vote in most European countries, Ireland gained its independence of Britain, the League of Nations was born and the United States of America emerged as the nation that could change world politics. The telephone replaced the telegraph and was available in every office and many middle class homes. The car became a commodity available to the middle classes too. The world was becoming a smaller place.

Twentieth century experiments with communism in Russia and capitalism in the West did not see the dream of material wealth for all come true. The depressions of the thirties led to a degree of poverty in Europe not experienced in a hundred years. The rise of the fascist movement, and its gaining of power in Germany and the resulting Second World War, shocked the civilized world. The horrors of not only modern mechanised warfare, but the nightmare of the holocaust undermined trust in governments and authority. The Vatican did not escape unscathed. Its sympathies with the right wing during the war left many a Catholic unhappy with the Pope and his leadership. European empires were collapsing, and with varying degrees of reluctancy on the part of European powers, new countries became independent of their colonial masters.

For the man or woman in the European street, however, a new prosperity was to dawn. The post war Atlee Labour government in Britain introduced social reforms without taking away all forms of free enterprise. The railways remained in public ownership as did the Post Office (which then included telephones) and the BBC and other forms of communication which were made available to all. By 1959 the Prime Minister, Harold McMillan was able to declare, "We're never had it so good!".

The Swinging Sixties and Beyond

The "swinging sixties" witnessed a freedom of choice in the West never before seen. There was a spirit of experiment and a sense of the ability to choose. Education, and (in Britain) free university places and maintenance grants meant new opportunities for young people in areas of life their fathers could not have dreamed of for themselves. On moral questions young people were engaged in debates about what was right and wrong on the merits of the cases to be made, rather than who made them. To their parents' alarm, people were asking "why?" as well as "what?". The pop music scene presented new choices of music with lyrics, hairstyles, clothes and a general lifestyle that were highly disturbing to the establishment. The response of young people was to revolt by imitating their pop heroes. Girls, perhaps, manifested more determination to revolt than boys – mini-skirts and trousers both made statements of a desire to break free from domesticity. Girls were seeking careers or higher education as a matter of course, and the "pill" enabled them to engage in sexual relationships without the risk of pregnancy. The "Summer of Love" of 1967 was a watershed.[23] The age of choice had established itself; former trust in, or obedience to, authority had passed. In 1968 the student strike that began at Nanterre in Paris confirmed this. This was a new revolution that spread beyond the student campuses to involve the workers too. In the same year the people overthrew the communist government in Czechoslovakia (the Prague Spring) even though it was rapidly put down by an armed Soviet response. In America there was huge opposition to the Vietnam war with many young people choosing prison rather than participation.

The churches were moving too, but institutions such as the Roman Catholic Church and national churches, such as the Church of England, are solid structures with central leaderships that tend to seek to maintain unity and cohesiveness. Pope John XXIII called the Second Vatican Council (1962-1965) which was to have a spirit of *aggionamento* (making the Church the Church of today). Huge strides were taken in terms of authority, liturgy (the language of the people should be used in place of Latin) and ecumenical relations. At the conclusion of the Council the Pope exchanged his triple tiara crown of regal authority for that of a mitre emphasising his pastoral role. But, in practice, the authority of the Council was limited and many conservatives rejected it. Pope Paul VI in was put into a corner in 1967 over the question of birth control. In 1931 Pius XI had expressly forbidden this in his encyclical *Casti Conubii.* Was the present Pope, in the spirit of reform brought about by Vatican Two, about to take a step (even a small one by saying, for example, that in certain circumstances it was permissible) that would change the edict of a former Pope? The answer was the encyclical *Humanii Vitae* which wholly affirmed the conservative stance. The hopes of many Catholics were dashed. Theologians were thrown into opposition of the Church, and many young people, seeking to limit the number of children they had, simply disobeyed the ruling. The age of choice had left the Roman Catholic Church in a siding. In the 1970s young people were increasingly ceasing to worship altogether, and clergy, monks and nuns left their orders in droves.

The Church of England, revised its liturgy – but it was not until 1980 that a complete prayer book was available that used modern English. Even then it was seen as the *"Alternative" Prayer Book.* Theologians and forward looking leaders within the church, even brave attempts by its General Synod, such as the Tiller Report on the pattern of ministry seem to have faded into oblivion. Monolithic churches, having to pay attention to traditional pressure groups, and the need to maintain and finance the organization, again have not the place they once had at the centre of society, determining its thought and morals. For many in Europe today, churches have become, Catholic and Protestant alike, alternatives to look into occasionally, to buy into when it suits, providers of some of the choices on offer. They are still, however, treated with caution and distrust.

An Unprecedented Rate of Change

If the speed of change is dependent on the speed of communication the invention and common distribution of the computer is indicative of the choices available in the present day. Within twenty years of the launch of desktop computers in the early 1980s, the vast majority of young people are computer literate in Europe having access to a variety of software and, above all, the Internet which provides them with any information they desire at the touch of a few buttons. Students can access sites from anywhere in the globe, and upload their own information. If the bicycle enabled people to meet those living within a fifty mile radius of their homes in the late 19th century, then the late 20th century equivalent is the current information exchange technology. Marriages may be "made in heaven" but, one of the latest weddings I have been privileged to conduct as a clergyman was a result of contact through a lonely hearts Internet site through which two people living two hundred miles apart conducted a successful courtship.

If we were to plot the opportunities for freedom of choice on a graph beginning in the Middle Ages what we see is, at first, a slow climb for the better off, with hardly anything for the common people. This increases sharply for the more educated with the advent of the printing press in the fifteenth century and the Reformation. Commoners moved with those who led their part of the world. The inclination of the graph continues to increase through the Enlightenment and into the 19th century, when the ordinary people feel the impact of change and choices with the onset of the Industrial Revolution. The 20th century shows the most rapid increase of choice available in any period of history, with the last 40 years seeing such a steep curve that it is difficult to plot. We are far from being able to say that nothing is really different these days, that every generation has seen changes, that we can carry on as we have always done. It amazes me just how many among whom I move take that line. Some are too old to desire to make the effort to understand, others are in strong denial, while yet others are taking the fundamentalist route resisting all change, adopting a beleaguered attitude to the world that surrounds them. But a huge number of those who have encountered contemporary culture, long to share their Good News of the God that has set them free with the world. It's these people that need the most help. Where, and how should they begin? We must start with gaining a deeper understanding of what it means to live in the world of infinite choice that we have today.

3. Current Cultural Trends in the Western World – A Paradox

The rate of change in current society is such that things are changing faster than they can be comprehended or, indeed, before most people have accessed the latest thing or idea. In January 2004 I changed my mobile phone for something that was even more compact and complex than the one I had before. In May 2004 I had just about understood some of what it could do, but by then the company had a completely new range and I was offered a "trade in" so that I could access the latest 3D technology. However did we manage without the silicon semi-conductor? Computer software is often out of date before it is marketed. The same is true in clothes fashions, music and all sorts of consumer goods. Not only medical treatment but the whole ethos of medicine and its relationship to patients has changed. Best practice in teaching has been revolutionized beyond recognition. The same applies to ideas and scholarship. In the fields of historical or religious studies (things that don't appear to have short shelf lives) lecturers often warn their students not to trust anything written more than twenty years ago.[24] Darwin was a best seller for over thirty years – something that would be difficult to imagine in the scientific world today.

Innovation at this pace has led to two opposing tendencies. On the one hand the proliferation of ideas has been given an ever widening amount of choice leading to the breakdown of monolithic systems and worldviews. The solid things that appear to have been there for ever are all being questioned – the world is becoming very fluid. However, on the other hand the very uncertain nature of a fluid world has increased the desire for unity and simplicity. Both these things are happening at the same time but, opposed as they are, they are not often the cause of conflict among many young people. These developments are happening alongside each other even within the minds and hearts of individuals. Where conflicts do occur is in those places where people deliberately resist change, or attempt to drive it in a given direction. The tendencies I am referring to here are often unconscious, underlying cultural currents. On one side we have the drift to pluralism, postmodernism, post-structuralism, and some semiological interpretation, that acclaims freedom of expression and discourages affiliation or commitment. "Reality" and "truth" are difficult concepts in this world. On the other side, the desire to live in a world that is not fractured and futile leads to a search for unified meaning epitomised by the search for a Grand Unified Theory (GUT) in physics, a global unity of purpose reflected in international relations – a longing for peace and harmony. Here we have ideas such as the Gaia Principle, environmental conventions such as the Kyoto Protocol, and calls for a super-moral order The way these sides come together is in expressions such as, "I want to be free to chose, of my own volition, to be a brother or sister to my neighbour". This sounds easy, but at every stage in practice it is open to unconscious misunderstanding, or deliberate exploitation and abuse. It shifts the responsibility from the community, where enforcement has often been the norm, to the individual. It requires trust and honesty in a world where many people regard those virtues as weaknesses to be taken advantage of. Nevertheless "democracy" and individual human rights (as, for example, those declared by the National Assembly of France in 1789)[25] have gained the respect of the Western world and have become part of the cultural landscape.

Postmodernism – a Fluid World

Rather than a movement that succeeded Modernism, Postmodernism is a rejection of the basic tenets of Modernism. Postmodernists draw their inspiration from every age of scholarship and thought and reject the Modernist concept of linear development. Modernism grew out of the underlying principles of the Enlightenment which believed that knowledge would eventually – however long it took – be able to provide an explanation for everything. Not only science but moral and social advancements would be made. Modernism makes "Progress" its goal and believes in it. The assumptions that govern Modernism are epitomized in the television series *Startrek* where the "Federation" is at peace, unity and harmony within itself, and human conflict on Earth is something that is only known in history books, whilst science has progressed to the point at which known illnesses can all be cured and people can travel faster than the speed of light. As we will see, Modernism is still, in a non-linear way, far from being old hat. The continuing contributions of science have meant that most people have not completely lost faith in progress. Yet postmodernist thinking colours our culture today, especially among the young.

Although, by its very nature, it is difficult to define Postmodernism, Tim Woods summarizes its characteristics as follows:

1. the undercutting of an all-encompassing rationality;
2. an incredulity towards metanarratives and a challenge to totalizing discourse, which is a suspicion of any discursive attempts to offer a global or universalist account of existence;
3. a rejection of modernism. (Woods: 10)

Metanarratives are defined by the *Free On-line Dictionary of Philosophy*[26] as "stories employed to legitimate the mechanisms of social control". That is stories that convey basic premises about the world and existence that new generations are not allowed to question. Roger Jones describes it thus:

> The postmodern subject has no rational way to evaluate a preference in relation to judgements of truth, morality, aesthetic experience or objectivity. As the old hierarchies of thought are torn down, a new clearing is formed on the frontiers of understanding: quite what hybrids of thought will metamorphose, interbreed and grow is this clearing is for the future to decide. (http://www.philosopher.org.uk)

Traditional ideas and systems from this point of view are seen as "constructs" – systems that are based and constructed on modernist principles or religious or other dogma for example. But it goes further than this because all sorts of inductive conclusions in science or historical and literary scholarship are called into question. In a postmodernist world no-one can be sure of anything, and reality itself becomes a problem. Jean Baudrillard, a french postmodern philosopher, is concerned with semiology (or semiotics). He believes that signs and models obscure reality because it is merely the sign we are aware of. The "model" determines what the real is and all we are left with is "hyperreality". The world becomes a series of "simulcra" (deceptive substitutes) that refer to nothing in real life. In his book *The Illusion of the End* inspired by the coming of the year 2000 (itself a human construct of course) Baudrillard argues that time has no linear reality, so cannot end.

> In the Euclidean space of history, the shortest path between two points is the straight line, the line of Progress and Democracy. But this is only true of the linear space of the Enlightenment. In our non-Euclidean *fin de siècle* space, a baleful curvature unfailingly deflects all trajectories. This is doubtless linked with the sphericity of time (visible on the horizon of the end of the century, just as the earth's sphericity is visible on the horizon at the end of the day) or the subtle distortion of the gravitational field.
>
> Ségalen says that once the Earth has become a sphere, every movement distancing us from a point by the same token also begins to bring us closer to that point. This is true of time as well. Each apparent movement of history brings us imperceptibly closer to its antipodal point, if not indeed to its starting point. This is the end of linearity. In this perspective, the future no longer exits. (Baudrillard,10).

In this kind of world there is no longer any room for God or the promise of life to come:

> " ... there are no longer any causes, *but only effects*. The world is there *effectively*. There is no reason for this, and God is dead. If nothing exists now but effects, we are in a state of total illusion ... If the effect is in the cause or the beginning in the end, then the

> catastrophe is behind us ... The end of the anticipatory psychoses, all panic, all remorse! The lost object is behind us. We are free of the Last Judgement. (Baudrillard,121)

Postmodernism invades all disciplines. It is seen in religious studies, history, art, linguistics, architecture and science. It is playing a transforming role in women's studies too. Among older people feminism is often regarded as a fairly recent phenomenon. In fact it came to prominence at the end of the nineteenth century and has slowly gained ground over the last hundred years. It has born fruit in abundance, however, in the last thirty years in all areas of life and the relationship of young men and women today assume far less gender differences than previous generations. Women will tell us that there is still some way to go. Nevertheless feminism is basically a product of the Enlightenment and is not immune from current postmodern trends. Michelle Barrett and Anne Phillips have edited a book entitled, *Destabilizing Theory* in which they trace the feminist debate in the postmodern and post-structuralist age. They comment:

> One of the issues here is whether feminism can survive as a radical politics if it gives up on a hierarchy of theory. Feminists have moved from a grand theory to local studies, from cross-cultural analysis of patriarchy to the complex and historical interplay of sex, race and class, from notions of female identity or the interests of women towards the instability of female identity and the active creation and recreation of women's needs or concerns. Part of what drops out in these movements is the assumption of a pre-given hierarchy of causation waiting only to be uncovered. Do such developments then leave feminists with nothing to say?

To someone like me who was an undergraduate in the late 1960s all this is new. Many of the books and lectures in those days have now been out of date for a long time. It is possible for older generations to dismiss Baudrillard and his ilk as off-centre and unimportant to the "normal" world. But philosophy, sociology, cultural studies and linguistics are all popular with current students. Throughout British universities books by Baudrillard, for example, are on short loan, and often provision is made by stocking multiple copies. His impact, and that of his postmodern friends such as Jean-François Lyotard, Jacques Derrida and Michel Foucault in the French speaking world is even more widespread. Postmodernism is not only articulated in pure philosophical study but is expressed through the arts, music, theatre and architecture. This thinking is having a huge impact on the way our intelligent young people view the world, faith and religion. It also has consequences for the unspoken general culture of younger people – even those who do not necessarily reflect academically about anything.

Among the more intellectual youngsters there is a search for meaning, purpose and reality – and perhaps a serious place for humanity in the universe. Responses to this come from scientific as well as religious quarters. Whilst politics and business have to work for the medium and short term, both science and religion can afford to focus on the long term. Political parties need to impress within a very few years if they wish to maintain (or gain) power; business has to get a return on its ventures in as short a time as possible or share-holders will remove their capital and invest elsewhere. Religion, however, despite the pressures to enter into this type of market culture in order to maintain (even increase) membership and income, is looked to by many for its prophetic witness to truths that transcend the everyday hurley-burly of life. Science, in ways that now go beyond the mechanistic ideas of the Enlightenment, can provide far reaching explanations and suggest systems in which the fragments of life can come together in a simple but all-embracing "theory of everything". Perhaps here, at last, is solid ground in a "liquid" world.

Unifying Theories

The search for the Theory of Everything (TOE) is not a new idea. It dates back to the early days of the Enlightenment, and is, therefore, a continuation of the Modernist dream. It is evidence that not all faith has been lost in the search for progress. In 1758 Roger Boscovich in his *Theory of Natural Philosophy* attempted a hypothesis in which a single law gave rise to all known phenomena. Much has been discovered since then but the principle is the same. Today's search for a Grand Unified Theory seeks to provide one single equation to encompass the four forces of nature – gravity, electromagnetism and the strong and weak nuclear forces that hold atoms together.[27] If this can be done it will provide information about the origin and structure of the universe that will change all scientific approaches to life. Many of those who have been working on this for years, have however, begun to doubt whether such a theory can ever be found. Intriguing suggestions have come forward that could provide explanations but, as yet, no-one has managed to complete both the maths and the laboratory testing that enable them to be verified. Nevertheless an idea in which our universe is one of many universes like bubbles within an infinite multiverse, where the vacuum is constantly spawning new universes, each with its own big bang, has sold many books to the general public as well as among physicists. The first sentence in a website (entitled *Keep it Real*)[28] dedicated to the theory introduces the topic thus: "So-called "Level I" (cosmological) and "Level III" (quantum mechanical) multiverses are in fact differing conceptual models of the same physical reality."

Another unified theory is "string theory" in which everything is considered to consist of infinitesimally small loops of twisted superstrings in six (or in some cases twenty-two) dimensions in addition to the observable ones of length, breadth, depth and time. One of the proponents of superstring theory, Edward Witten,[29] Professor of Physics at the Institute of Advanced Study, Princeton, New Jersey, describes it as beautiful. Employing hypotheses with names like supersymmetry and harmonics on "fundamental strings" appeals to people in a confused world. String theory admits to a "fuzziness of spacetime" but, from which, emerges a unifying theory that underlies all that is.

This includes consciousness. Whilst we may be able to indicate ways in which the laws of physics control the way particles behave, or even how DNA enables those particles to ensure the growth of systems that can be described as "alive", the question of how consciousness arises still needs to be answered. How is it that certain combinations of quarks, neutrinos, atoms and complex molecules gives an individual the ability to be aware of him/herself and reflect on the world in which we live? Dinah Zohar in her book *The Quantum Self* comes up with a theory that "transcends the dichotomy between body and mind":

> ... the basic building blocks of mind (bosons) and the basic building blocks of matter (fermions) arise out of a common, quantum substrate (the vacuum) and are engaged in a mutually creative dialogue whose roots can be traced back to the very heart of reality creation. Crudely put, mind is relationship and matter is that which it relates. Neither on its own could evolve or express anything, together they give us ourselves and the world. (Zohar, 218).

Zohar is anxious to deliver the world from an idea that science stands aloof from "we conscious human beings". She wishes to deliver us from being "somehow strangers in the universe, merely an accidental by-product of blind evolutionary forces with no particular role to play in the scheme of things..." (Zohar, 1). Zohar is not alone in this; similar work is being done at the interfaces of the departments of quantum physics and psychology in many of our institutions.

For non-scientists like myself reading this work, it is hard not to believe we are in a world of science-fiction. But this is not fiction at all, it is serious scientific work being done by foremost scientists in our leading universities across the world. It is important for us, in the context of this book, because it indicates the direction in which human beings are prepared to commit their energy and intellect. Funding for these projects could only come from those who have the imagination to go beyond the self-centred choice of short-term gain and look for something that will eventually bring us together in some kind of glorious unity. Early in 2005 a new book is due to be published entitled: *God the Multiverse and Everything: Modern Cosmology and the Argument from Design.*[30] God features strongly in all this. The more science advocates "keeping it real" with an increasing number of dimensions, and the more cosmologists, quantum physicists and mathematicians marvel at the beauty of the world/universe/multiverse, the more room there is for a divine Creator that both transcends it and in-dwells it. As we marvel at the laws of physics and seek a unified theory, the question will always arise: Are these laws a pure accident or is there a Grand Designer behind it all?

In today's, pressured, short-term, multi-choice, everyday Western world scientists and theologians find themselves on the same side. Both are delighting in the beauty of matter, mind and the human spirit. Both are speaking prophetically about the dangers of consumption, exploitation, oppression and ignorance.

Concern for Planet Earth

If there is a conflict between short-term and long-term interests in the world, one of its most acute battle grounds is in relation to the environment. The more scientists discover about our planet, the more they are aware of the necessity of careful balance. The rows about what scientists can really tell us, or what is bunkum revolve around two major facts. The first is that science has to be funded, and that funding often comes from those looking for short-term gain (the business circle and politicians). The second is that, whilst science cannot predict with certainty the precise individual outcomes of our present degree of exploitation of the environment, it is bound to have an effect. The environment could become unbalanced if we continue to release carbon and other substances from fossil reserves into the atmosphere whilst the planet is deforested. Nor can we afford to ignore human exploitation of other human beings on a global scale. Contemporary technology leaves us all vulnerable to social pressures only known before at local levels.

The Gaia Hypothesis grew from an insight by James Lovelock in the 1960s.[31] He noticed that the atmosphere and mean temperature of the Earth appeared to be self-regulating. On discussing his theories with the novelist William Golding, the latter suggested the name Gaia (after the Greek Earth goddess) for his hypothesis. The constant salinity of the oceans has since been quoted as an indicator of this. If we define life as a network which constantly makes itself, then it is as if the planet were itself a living organism that can maintain itself for the benefit of all the life that thrives upon it. Lovelock describes his hypothesis by imagining a planet which has only two species of life – light daisies and dark daisies. This is his Daisyworld. The light daisies reflect light while the dark daisies absorb it. If the sun's luminosity increases, the light daisies increase in number replacing dark daisies to maintain the balance of temperate that favours the growth of daisies. The system regulates itself. "Daisyworld", says David Orrell, "addresses the dichotomy that exists between the reductionist approach, which attempts to understand systems by breaking them down to their smallest components, and the holistic approach which views systems as complete entities that must be understood in their entirety". Orrell concludes:

> One of the lessons of Daisyworld is that, due to the effect known as hysteresis, damage once done is very difficult to undo. Our experiment with global warming cannot be halted when we are uncomfortable with the effects; by then it may be too late. And once a species is extinct, it cannot be restored. We are just one part of a larger system, and are reliant on that system for our continued existence. We harm it at our peril.[32]

There is an increasing number of people who believe this and who are determined to do something about it. Whilst they do not have the power to take control away from the capitalist system that regulates global trade they can, and are, having a significant influence upon it. Christian Aid's slogan "We believe in life before death" reflects where many people, especially young people, believe religion should be. It is crucial for proponents of faith, they believe, to avoid the impression that they are about "pie-in-the-sky-when-you-die" and thus appear to collude with short-term exploitation by turning a blind eye. Faith should empower people, not silence them. It is important to note that for those who have a concern for environmental protection and human justice, religious people who claim a relationship with God and who proclaim him as Creator should, at first sight at any rate, appear to have something in common. There are indeed, if not yet mainstream, movements within Christianity in particular in which these issues are promoted. I have already mentioned Christian Aid. There is a huge Christian contribution to other relief agencies as well, both large and small. Christian ecology links promote ways in which local churches can do "green things" ranging from supermarket petitions for ethically produced goods[33] to managing churchyards.[34] Celtic spirituality, which is becoming increasingly popular, enables people to connect with nature in a mystical way – a way that appears to connect with something that is already there within the unconscious.[35] In these areas religion and science have combined forces to campaign for the long view, whilst at the same time claiming that for some individuals (especially in the third world) a change in emphasis from profit to philanthropic concern will make an immediate impact.

Although in practice Western lifestyles have a lot more changing to do, the principle of the need for change for the long-term has been increasingly acknowledged. It is a lobby that cannot be ignored even by presidents and prime-ministers, and forms an important focus of unity within a fragmented world of personal choice. America lags behind in this, and it is chiefly the attitude of the USA, in refusing to ratify it, that has made the 1997 Kyoto Protocol something for which we are not yet all aspiring, but especially among the educated young people of Western Europe, there is a growing ground-swell of support.

The tragedy of this is that the while we may be making progress we are still continuing to damage our planet even though we may be sure of the need to change. Will we be able to change the aspirations of the those seeking short-term gain in time? Perhaps in Europe strong political leadership that sees governments basing their policies primarily on environmental and justice issues may actually come off. In America, however, it may still have some way to go. Perhaps, in the end like so many other things, it will depend on the vested interests of the media and multinational corporations – or just simple selfish collective desire.

Current Perceptions and Future Hope

In an interesting analysis written in 1992, Julian Simon believes that things have been and are getting better for individuals.[36] The perception, however, is different. Statistics reveal that as we have become more proficient in health and safety, and have been increasingly aware of the dangers of natural disasters in certain areas and take measures to meet them, there have been fewer life threatening disasters from decade to decade. He predicts that will continue. The future will concern fewer struggles against nature and more battles between human groups (Simon, 655). On the whole, where conflicts have been avoided or controlled, conditions have got better. Yet perceptions have got worse. Some of this has something to do with the media. Simon tells a story of his mother:

> A curiosity: My mother ... was born in 1900 and saw her only child saved from death at age seven by the first new wonder drug. In her eighties she knew that her friends had mostly lived extraordinarily long lives. She recognized the convenience and comfort provided by such modern inventions as the telephone, air-conditioning, and airplanes. And yet she disagreed when I said the conditions of life had markedly improved. When I asked Mother why she still thought things have gotten worse, she replied: 'The headlines in the newspapers are all bad.'" (Simon, 654-655)

I paid a recent visit to the Cotentin region of France, near Cherbourg. I had a very interesting visit to a school for young people especially designed for those destined to work as farm-workers, plumbers, builders and the like.[37] Most of them felt things were worse for them than their parents or grandparents. Their parents had not had to face the choices they were confronted with. Their elders had not had to gain qualifications and "bits of paper", the police were not so strict on motoring offences (especially related to drinking), there was more work in the countryside and the place wasn't so full of immigrants who were "stealing their jobs". Certainly employment prospects have changed, and there is a need for "bits of paper" but the life their parents led during and immediately after the war (an area decimated in the months leading up to, during and thirteen days after D-Day) where food, clothing and mod-cons were almost unattainable must have been worse. Their forebears may not have faced clamp downs on drinking and driving, but the alcohol would have been harder to get and far fewer ordinary people owned cars. Attention to health and safety didn't exist as it does today. They could not even imagine a world without televisions, computer games and chocolate! Women in the 1950s would have been expected to wash by hand and tend the garden plot. The life-style of young women in the region today far exceeds anything their grandmothers (even their mothers) could have imagined. And yet so many of the young people see the world in a negative way.

Some of this has to do with the media, and some to politics and big business. Adversarial politics lends itself to one party reporting on the failure of their rivals, and finding every opportunity to run down any progress made under their term of office. Health provision and education have improved enormously since I was a child, and yet public perceptions are different. Big business advertises bigger and better products – their future depends on people's desire to want what they produce – and to be dissatisfied with what they already have. We are back with those whose interest is to motivate people in the short-term. "Elect us!", "Buy from us!" they proclaim, and we gain our values from a media with so many vested interests in echoing those cries.

Many scientists and theologians and church leaders, looking to the long-term, believe science and religion have to resist being drawn into this clamour. Nevertheless both religion and science have their populists that assure us that propaganda is what is required. Extremists in both, but especially religion, are exceptionally good at it, because, whether they realize it or not, they are putting publicity before principle. Jacques Ellul believed that propaganda is one of the most serious threats to our world. In relation to the church he wrote:

> From the moment the church exposes itself to the conflict between sociological determinants and a contrary inspiration that comes from God and is directed towards God – from the moment the church uses propaganda and uses it successfully, it becomes, unremittingly, a purely sociological organization. It loses the spiritual part, for it now transmits only a false Christianity; it subordinates the essence of its being to sociological determination, in the world, and, in fact, it succeeds: it does become such a power. At that moment it has chosen power above truth. (Ellul 1973: 231).

The Modernist world was one in which people believed in progress. Today that has largely changed. People, for the reasons we have outlined, are much more cynical about the future. The postmodern world has introduced a sense of confusion and doubt with its emphasis on choice and indeterminism. We long to come together, to unite, to live at peace and yet we do not believe we can. Somehow Christians who believe in the power of the Holy Spirit of God to complete and unify the human spirit of individuals, communities and at global levels, must find a way of witnessing to that without succumbing to the pitfalls of propaganda.

"Creativity Born in Chaos": Solving the Paradoxes

For the rest of this chapter I want to talk of the work of Charles Handy in his book *The Empty Raincoat* published in 1994. Handy analyses the paradoxes of the world we live in and finds a way forward to hope. Although he is not a member of a faith community, Handy says, it is important to believe in something – to believe, "that we have something like a soul, that we matter, and that we are, in some small way, unique" (Handy, 239). He refers us to the white stone mentioned in the Book of Revelation: "Let anyone who has an ear listen to what the Spirit is saying to the churches. To everyone who conquers I will give some of the hidden manna, and I will give a white stone, and on the white stone is written a new name that no one knows except the one who receives it." (Rev. 2:17). The new name is that of Christ, written on a potsherd used to cast a vote for or against someone's continued inclusion in society. Cast out of society or persecuted, Christian disciples can continue on in the knowledge that they matter to God as unique individuals. Their names are written in the Lamb's Book of Life. If we don't believe we matter, continues Handy, "there will be no reason to do anything. The world would be at the mercy of all those who did believe that they could change things. It is a risk we cannot run." (Handy, 239). Handy refers us to Václav Havel:

> Is there a point to it all, and if so what is it? Václav Havel, the playwright turned president, could hardly be more immersed in worldly things and structures these days, but he has argued that we will only avoid 'mega-suicide' in our time if we rediscover a respect for something otherworldly, something beyond ourselves. It is a paradox, he says. but without that respect for a superpersonal moral order, we will not be able to create the social structures in which a person can truly be a person. (Handy, 3-4)

Handy no longer believes in a "theory of everything" as it refers to society. He believes paradox is inevitable and must be lived in. "Paradox has to be accepted, coped with and made sense of, in life, in work, in community and among the nations" (Handy, 18). He identifies nine paradoxes in the present world: intelligence, work, productivity, time, riches, organizations, age, the individual and justice. In each case they work for us and bring us benefits, but we are also at their mercy. We cannot ignore them, but must maintain some control. In the case of justice for example: " capitalism depends on the fundamental principle of inequality – some may do better than others – but will only be acceptable in the long term in a democracy if most people have an equal chance to aspire to that inequality. It is a paradox we cannot afford to ignore" (Handy, 43). So "we stand today at the crossroads, asking the way to our future. Words like hierarchy, loyalty and duty no longer carry the weight they once did. Other words like freedom, choice, and rights turn out to be more complicated than they seemed." (Handy, 54).

Central to Handy's thesis is the acceptance of change, and the preparedness for it. He describes a sigmoid curve – an "s" shaped curve on its back. Beginning in a trough and climbing to a climax before falling away again, the curve traces the graph of the process of development in all sorts of ventures in society – The clue to a successful organization, business, institution or project is the ability of its leaders to recognize that things need to change, need to be re-initiated, before the climax is reached. Re-investment or review needs to happen on the "up" because it is too late once the corner has been turned and people have begun losing faith in leaders, ideas or prospects. We can begin a new curve that will be a departure from the old one but will take over when the old one begins to decline. Too often, he believes, we leave things too late. Then it is necessary to retrench and begin again. This can be avoided if we re-invent what we are doing in time. In applying this to the world he declares: "It is tempting to think that the world has always been arranged the way it is and to delude ourselves that nothing will ever change. The discipline of the second curve keeps one sceptical, curious and inventive – attitudes essential in a time of change, and the best way of coping with the contradictions which accompany such a time." (Handy, 56). The Japanese have a term for the old guard who deny the changes. They are called "wet leaves" – they just stick around without any positive contribution. This theory can be applied to our institutions and corporations, but also to our personal careers and even family lives. For example, married partners should be prepared to embark on new ventures and explore new dynamics to their relationship. In this way relationships can stay fresh and avoid the destructiveness of failure. Handy is warning us that if we are to make a vibrant contribution to our world we should always have a positive sense of purpose. Handy observes that Allan Bloom[38] saw that the philosophy of Descartes (in which humanity is viewed as a small speck of dust in the universe) was making American college students:

> not only lifeless and ignorant, but reluctant to offer or to hold any opinions at all. People who thought they were right in the past did terrible things as a result, therefore it is best to have no opinions at all. The only true knowledge is science. Everything else is wishful

> thinking. From that it follows that it is wrong to take a position on anything, worse still to try and impose your wishes on your bit of the world. A passive voyeurism will have to suffice... (Handy, 238).

That way, believes Handy, lies a moral vacuum, "where nothing is right and nothing really wrong. That way lies inertia, no second curve, with compromises made for the wrong reasons – for a quiet life, not for justice, not for progress" (Handy, 238).

So we have to take the initiative in our confusing world, we have to work through and within the paradoxes of life and not allow ourselves to give up on each other. Progress has been made, it is possible and we can make the world a better place both now and in the future. We should actively encourage politicians with vision and courage, we should seek to become more deeply engaged with our world and lead others to do so too. Handy advocates what he calls "cathedral philosophy". The people who designed our great cathedrals did so knowing that they would not live long enough to see their projects completed. "We need to look beyond the grave and beyond our generation" (Handy, 242). "The hope lies in the unknown, in that second curve, if we can find it. The world is up for re-invention in so many ways. Creativity is born in chaos." (Handy, 270).

Charles Handy paints a picture in which humanity need not be at the mercy of dysfunctional trends. In recent polls concerning interest in politics and activism, the people he represents may still be a minority, but I believe they can, in the words of Jesus, be the "leaven in the lump" and that leaven need not be extremist or divisive but positive and inclusive. We need people to articulate what they mean by goodness, love, unity and peace – in fact in the "fruits of Spirit" as St. Paul calls them (Galatians 5) – in actions as well as words. As St. Paul indicates, Christians believe that God invests those who seek him with the power to transform community. Christians do not go it alone. All we need to do is be true to ourselves and our calling. If we are authentic then people will see that and respond accordingly. Christianity, I believe, has much that is relevant in our world today.

4. The Everyday World of Young People

Postmodernism calls into question basic assumptions of life received in the Western world since the Enlightenment and before. Young people no longer feel they can accept values and beliefs without question. When I was a child it was deemed rude to ask one's parents why one was not allowed to do something, or why we were expected to behave in a certain manner. The response, "Because I say so!" was all one was going to get from most parents. Today's children expect a satisfactory answer, and most parents don't believe the question 'why?' is necessarily rude – nor are they reluctant to admit they do not know. The best parents say, "Let's find out" and help the child explore. This is hard for some older people to come to terms with.

Young People and Freedom of Choice and Opportunity

There is the question of enjoyment. The old ideas of self denial seem pointless to most young people. It's not that they are reluctant to think of others – just that they need to be assured that it's necessary. They unconsciously live out the fourth human right enshrined in the French Declaration 1789: "Liberty consists in the freedom to do everything which injures no one else; hence the exercise of the natural rights of each man has no limits except those which assure to the other members of the society the enjoyment of the same rights". This is not a pure hedonism that ignores the needs of others, but it is certainly about enjoying life to the full, taking advantage of opportunities and doing the things they might be good at. They get little satisfaction out of dutiful sacrifice because few people, outside of radical sects, are going to admire them for it these days.

Then there is the question of choice. The postmodern world allows a pick-and-mix approach. People feel they can respond to that which attracts them and reject that which doesn't. This will not appeal to the purist, but most young people would not object to some-one mixing Eastern religion with a dash of Christianity on a bed of New Age paganism if that is what turns them on.

Young people are quite capable of holding more than one idea in their heads at the same time. Non-linear dynamics is not just a philosophical idea, it's is a way of life.[39] If quantum physics can have its Uncertainty Principle,[40] or acknowledge that light can be both particles and waves[41] at the same time, then we can hold on to different ways of interpreting the same processes in daily life too. The problem, for example, of reconciling the Genesis creation accounts with the theory of evolution belong to the modernist world. People of a postmodern disposition can hold the two things in an imaginative tension. Nor is the idea of a "Holy Trinity" in Christianity or the "two natures" (divine and human) of Christ something which bothers people like it did in the early to middle twentieth century. "Multi-tasking" is a common concept for those who work with computers (and that includes virtually all young people in Britain and Western Europe).

Above all it is the rapid pace of change and lack of cohesion and unpredictability about how the world will be tomorrow that invites a short-term, living-for-the-moment attitude to living. It discourages long term planning and commitment. Young people are prepared to move not only around the country but around the world. Our universities are international, and our streets echo with the sounds of many languages. The local pub now serves curry and Chinese dishes and offers Australian, American and continental beer alongside new and old world wines. Fashions come and go, and its tough deciding on what will be "cool" or "naff" tomorrow – and, sadly, that matters. A job is no longer a job for life – who knows whether that particular skill is going to be required next year (let alone ten years hence). Traditional marriage is put off while couples elect for provisional relationships and serial monogamy.[42] Even sexual orientation has become a matter of debate and choice since there is less and less social pressure to conform with traditional norms. For girls, choices are better then they were for their mothers. However, they are conscious of what is called the "glass ceiling"[43] and are prepared to have to fight harder than their male contemporaries.

In the midst of all this, however, and perhaps because of it, there is a real hankering after stability. Despite the reluctance among young people of any social background to commit themselves permanently to anything or anyone, there is a definite desire to identify with something that involves other people.

Disadvantaged Young People

It seems that young people move into two main "camps" at a fairly young age in their early teens. They are separated by their attitude to the postmodern world of choice. On the one hand there are those who rejoice in the opportunities that education and reduced discrimination afford them. They are motivated by success, and the encouragement they receive from teachers and older people in general. They work hard, sometimes excessively so. They enjoy the company of those likewise motivated. On the other hand, the choice based on academic or sporting achievement leaves those with low self-esteem to experience the world in a negative light. Those who are poor or who have suffered neglect or abuse are often trapped. In her book *Feminism and Youth Culture*, Angela Mc Robbie comments:

> The good fortune of affluent parents and a comfortable home can indeed mean that for young women there is now the strong possibility of high educational achievement and rewarding employment. But this rosy ideal is countered by the harsh reality of

> growing up in a low-income, lone parent household. In such a context the years between 16 and 18 (the A level period) put enormous if not unbearable pressure on poor homes. Working long hours in supermarkets or other low paid jobs, attending low-achieving schools and lacking the time and the expertise of parents with knowledge of the educational system still means that in such circumstances the odds are heavily stacked against the most brilliant pupil, male or female." (McRobbie, 199).

Many of these slip quickly into the use of alcohol, tobacco, sex and sometimes drugs. They seek easy, undemanding activities for quick thrills and often find themselves in trouble. They cannot see why society (often represented by the police and the courts) does not allow them to make the choices they wish to make. The world of young people is hugely diverse with a major rift between the motivated and those who drift, between those who have gained a sense of achievement through making meaningful choices among the opportunities they have, and those whose self-esteem is low. *Faith in The City* pointed to the truth that those who are live in Urban Priority Areas[44] just do not have the same chance as those who are residents of middle class, suburban households. That was 1985, and things are little better in some places. In fact the difference between the opportunities that are available to the better off youngster and the disadvantages of their poor neighbours have, if anything, widened. Karen Sternheimer speaks of "digital disempowerment". "According to a 2002 Annie E. Casey Foundation[45] study", she writes, "having access to a computer at home increases educational performance, even when factors like income are taken into a account." (Sternheimer, 204). Of course those with low incomes and cramped houses are the least likely to own a computer.

The more opportunities of choice the contemporary world throws up, the greater the frustration and the lower the self-esteem of the disadvantaged youngster becomes. For those in their teens searching for some kind of self identity such disadvantages put them at greater risk of slipping into despair and all that goes with it. One way in which young people who live on the edge of society deal with this is to belong to sub groups. In Britain these are variously named depending on where they live. They distinguish themselves by their dress and jewellery, the way they talk and walk and the music they listen to. Fairly wide spread are the "Goths" who dress in black and white clothes and sometimes have white faces. "Skaters" or "Skate-boys" (as they are called in the North-East) are never to be parted from their skate boards which have become a symbol of identity. "Pikies" wear caps with peaks set at forty-five degrees and short baggy trousers. In some parts of England similarly dressed youngsters who walk with their feet thrust out to the side, call themselves "Gangsters" and show a particular liking for rap music. "Grebs" go for baggy clothes and rock. Girls' gangs are on the increase too as females become more assertive, and "laddettes"[46] have become a recognised current phenomenon.

Not all young people, of course, belong to a particular sub-group. From the young people interviewed by Brannen, Dodd, Oakley and Storey, "In practice only a fifth of young people claim definite allegiances to a particular dress style" (Brannen, 26). Among working class men football is a common form of identity. They have their teams and their countries to cheer for – and sometimes get drawn into alcohol fuelled violence. Some young women become ardent followers of soap opera, music stars or screen actors. These people become their "cult heroes" and what they say and do is pondered over and imitated. Despite a world of choice young people want to be seen to be making the same choices as their peers.

It is important for young people to know themselves at a young age. I find youngsters as young as 13 able to articulate clearly what they wanted for themselves, what they believed was right for them, and why. In today's environment there is no way any parent or society can protect or isolate their young people from everything out there that's going. What's not on offer at school (and there's very little that isn't) or the television, can be had on the Internet. Young people know how they can get anything from drugs to pornography, and things that older people have no inkling even exist. Youngsters, therefore, are under a great deal of pressure from those who would exploit them. It is not possible to be "blissfully innocent" and they have to know why they like or dislike things. The pressures on youngsters – especially when they are 11 to 14 are immense. They come under pier pressures, fears about their appearance and acceptability, school work, and expectations of parents and older people in general. They are probably more aware of the dangers of anorexia than obesity. They have choices to make regarding what they approve of and what they don't, the ways they are going to take and the paths they are going to reject. This demands courage and determination, and risks bullying and isolation.

Relationships with Older People

Older people, especially those that grew up in the harder times when choices were limited by the 1930s depression and the war and its aftermath, find themselves in a strange land in today's fluid world. They rejoice in the new security that peace and prosperity have brought and find it hard to understand why so many young people should be so unhappy. "If we only had half what these teenagers have these days we'd have been over the moon", said one old gentleman. Of course he would. Young people can see that, in a detached way. They have done their history lessons and most would not like to go back into the 1930s and 40s, but that does not mean they do not have problems themselves nowadays that older people did not have when they were young. The freedoms of today pose frightening scenarios that older people never had to face. A world of choice can be very alarming, especially if you don't wish to be left out, overlooked or rejected. Take, for example, the girl who, at the age of 23 still remembered clearly the new pair of trainers her grandmother insisted on buying her when she was fifteen. These were reduced in price, "a real bargain" the grandmother said. They were "perfectly good shoes" – but they were not the kind in which girls of her age would want to be seen! The grandmother couldn't understand this. For her to have a "decent" pair of shoes to wear was what counted – it would have done "when *she* was young!" To her a "decent" pair meant "without holes", "serviceable" or "new". To the fifteen year old "decent" means something else that can be roughly translated as "cool", something that would recommend them to other people of her age. The grandmother was interested in practicalities, but the granddaughter needed to make the right kind of choice in a tough world. So the girl wore the shoes at home, but took them off before she went out. A grandparent's remark, "I just don't understand young people these days", is an accurate one. It is interesting to note that, when viewed the other way round young people, on the whole, understand older generations more than older people imagine. But young people are not part of their "pre-postmodern" world.

Sometimes old people feel that the young have rejected them. For most young people that is not true. They are keen to hear their stories and tales of what they did in the past. They enjoy being part of a family which contains people that are settled and know themselves, and they want to hear what old people think about the ultimate questions of life and what they make of God and hope. Most young people like being appreciated and wanted for themselves and loved, and they value older people who try to see what it is like for them. My wife and I have been most privileged to meet many young people both where we live and through a sabbatical tour in the Spring of 2004, and to explore with them what they feel are the challenges they face. To avoid the fear that we were going to be judgemental we chose the name "The Listening People". We have been impressed with just how much young people want to talk, how much they want to know, and how interested they are in what we are doing and believing. The majority of young people are not happy with a generation gap, and many of them try quite hard to understand where older people "are coming from". It is equally important for older people to have the insight and the courage to reach out and seek to understand what it's like for young people in a postmodern world. Whether we like it or not, this world is not going to revert to Victorian values (or virtues, as they would have called them) no matter how much "grey power" is applied. If people wish to live according to former lights then that is their choice – but they have to remember that it is a choice made possible by a postmodern society that allows such choices. And in such a society they cannot hope to impose it upon others.

What young people most enjoy about older people is when they talk about their experiences honestly and openly. They like stories of what it used to be like, and are genuinely interested in people's experience of the Second World War, for example, or ways of doings things before so many mod-cons appeared on the scene. Many young people have very good relationships with most, if not all, of their family members and delight in their grandparents. The picture changes, however, when they encounter older people in general.

A major problem that some young people have towards older generations is the fear of being unjustly judged. There comes across to them a mixture of disapproval and resentment. Modes of dress, life-styles and sexual behaviour come in for censure and condemnation. But just because someone wears holey jeans or uses a skate board does not mean they are immoral and out of control. Nor does the fact that young people mostly elect to live together before marriage mean that that they are "loose", irresponsible or "living in sin". (I would suggest that the emphasis in the past on "carnal lusts" has been out of proportion compared with the blind eye often turned to the sins of gossip, oppression and manipulation of power). In a fluid society, which says that everyone should be permitted his or her own choice of life-style so long as it does not impinge on the freedom of others, young people cannot see how their low-cut jeans or pierced navels affect other generations – after all they don't try to stop them wearing the old fashioned clothes and jewellery old people like. It is not that young people don't judge or make value judgements. They are not opposed to being judged (any more than anyone else), but if they are judged they want to be judged according to the values of the 21st century rather than a "black and white" world of the past that old people insist on clinging to. This is a world that comes out in expressions such as, "When I was young ..." or, "I don't know what things are coming to these days ...".

Young people object to being compared with former generations. They dislike older people justifying themselves by putting down the young. A universal cry, I meet, is that young people feel that some older people regard all young people as being the same, and assume they are all bad. Brannen writes, "Teenagers are less likely than their parents to generalize and they prefer to judge and be judged on an individual basis" (Brannen, 24). They are concerned that older people judge their morality solely on the way they dress or the jewellery they wear. It does not follow automatically that the appearance of a young person means that they are immoral or unhelpful. Young people do not find it easy to meet one another casually or socially.[47] They live in houses shared by their families, and private meeting places are often not open to them. They worry about the way that older people react to them when they meet in public places, assuming that they are "up to no good" and sometimes calling the police. If young people are not allowed to meet in public places where are they to go? Everywhere belongs to some-one else, and they don't have the resources to pay to "get into" places all the time. It is the nature of youth to desire to meet other youngsters informally to debate, court and play and this often involves groups large enough to have several smaller sub-groups through which different members can pass as in, for example, a dance or a party. Clubs or venues can be prohibitively expensive. Parks, public gardens and town centres provide free locations. Unfortunately loud minorities do sometimes abuse these places but managing the disruptive individuals would seem preferable to banning all young people from meeting in public places at all.[48]

It appears that old people sometimes physically push young people around. The bus queue was mentioned more than once where old people use their weight to get on the bus in front of young people. Sometimes young people are jostled in the street. "They take advantage of the fact that I can't push back", said one. Verbal abuse is not uncommon. It appears that some older people feel they are in competition with the young and need to assert themselves. (The same is especially so when race is a factor).

Many older people exhibit a fear of the young. Because they do not understand them, especially in the mass, they often shun them – even avoiding places where they congregate. If they meet in large enough numbers the police are sometimes called for, even when nothing unlawful is taking place. The media contribute to this in alarming headlines and the use of inflammatory words such as "hoodlums", and "louts". Angela McRobbie recalls the "moral panics" of the late 1980s and 1990s. She writes that moral panics, "are a means of orchestrating consent by actively intervening in the space of public opinion and social consciousness through the use of highly emotive and rhetorical language which has the effect of requiring that 'something be done about it'. The argument about deviancy amplification is precisely that where such strategies are indeed followed by social and legislative action, they also reassure the public that there is strong government and strong leadership." (McRobbie, 180). She describes moral panics as those anxieties that, "involve the immorality of young people, the absence of parental control, the problem of too much free time leading to crime, and the threat that deviant behaviour poses to national identity and labour discipline." (McRobbie, 182-183). Fortunately, in recent years it seems there is less of a tendency to over-react (for example, on behalf of the police).

One of the main things that older people have always worried about in the young is their sexual behaviour. The past has always seemed more innocent. Somehow people seem to think that the young today are doing things they would never have dreamed of doing. It is true that young people, on the whole, have more opportunities for sexual encounters than in the past, but that does not mean they are any less moral or less wise. Karen Sternheimer urges: "We ought to stop whining about what young people shouldn't know and start dealing with what they *do* know. Adults should focus on enriching, rather restricting young people's knowledge about sex." (Sternheimer, 177).

Despite what older people believe, their expectations of our young people are not the same as they were for former generations. We can no longer expect boys to go to work at 14 and girls to stay at home until they marry. Indeed many of those we speak about today in disparaging tones as "teenage mothers" may well have left home and been married in former times. So, says Sternheimer, "socially and sexually we expect teenagers today to function partially as adults and partially as children. The roles and expectations of adolescents today are far different from their counterparts a hundred years ago." (Sternheimer, 172). The term "teenager" was first used by G. Stanley Hall in 1904. It is difficult for these teenagers to fulfil all the expectations of their elders. Joseph Damrell explains, "Youth are enjoined to take life easy, but not to cultivate bad habits; to live for the moment, but at the same time act responsibly; to get involved in the world around them, but not so involved that the call of duty, when it comes, will not be heard." (Damrell, 216). But what do young people expect of themselves?

Hopes and Fears of Young People

Patrick Heaven reports a 1986 survey by Newcomb, Huba and Bentler of over a thousand teenagers. They were asked to indicate their most desired life events and their least desired events. From talking to young people they haven't changed much. What they enjoyed most were the things that gave them a sense of achievement and a measure of independence. What they least desired concerned failures in family matters over which they had no control but which impinged greatly upon them.

Most Desired event:	Least desired event
1. Started driving	1. Got or gave VD
2. Got own stereo or TV	2. Death in family
3. Making some money	3. Serious accident or illness
4. Fell in love	4. Family accident or illness
5. Started dating regularly	5. Had a gay experience
6. Met a teacher I liked a lot	6. Trouble with the law
7. Holidayed without parents	7. Parents abused alcohol
8. Joined a club or group	8. Parents argued or fought
9. Decided about uni or college	9. Thought about suicide
10. Got religion	10. Family money problems

In 2004 we probably need to substitute "stereo" with "ipod" or "3D phone", and in the least desired list "parents separated or divorced" should appear fairly high up. Even "gained a step-parent" would probably be in the negatives list for some teenagers.[49] In one church I visited the young people had made drawings that traced their life stories to the present time. One young lady told us about her swimming and dancing and her progress through primary and secondary schools, her trips abroad and musical achievements. In the centre of her path were her exam successes and her hopes for university entry in the Autumn. Her's was a road of success. Others had successes in different ways and all were positive. The church group was clearly an affirming community that not all young people have the good fortune to enjoy.

It is interesting that "got religion" appears in the list of the ten most desirable life events. Most young people probably wouldn't put it that way but where they come across a life changing encounter with God it is probably the biggest thing that has happened to them. Because Christianity addresses the heart of self image and personal worth it can be a springboard for an unanticipated blossoming of life. I have come across young people who had virtually given up on life – sometimes involving a cycle of alcohol, drugs, self-harming and eating disorders – for whom life has taken on a new meaning. It is now time to look at the riches God offers, and the hope in which we rejoice.

5. God, Christianity and the 21st Century World view

Fewer literate people are familiar with Scripture in the 21st century in Europe than in any previous generation. The simple fact that the Bible is divided into two Testaments is something new to many young people. Even older people, when faced, for example, with Biblical questions on programmes such as ITV's *Who wants to a Millionaire?,* often do not know where to begin. The excitement that people show when reading passages of the Bible, sometimes for the first time, is a privilege to witness. There is no doubt that, given the opportunity, and a little help to know how to begin with a complex series of books containing millions of words, the Scriptures have a resonance and relevance in our postmodern world. I am reminded of a French couple who had joined a new diocesan Christian formation course that included studying the Bible. With the help of Charpentier's, *How to Read the Old Testament,* they had tackled large chunks of it. The study meeting had become highlights of their week and their excitement bubbled over into their conversation with their friends.

Different aspects of Scripture speak to various people in their own circumstances. In the late 1970s teaching Religious Knowledge to disenfranchised (and often disaffected) young Aborigines in Australia, I became aware of a real interest in the Exodus stories. These young teenagers had no knowledge of what was happening in South America and Southern Africa where Liberation Theology was enabling local communities to make sense of their world, but they were instantly attracted to the same passages of Scripture. Through that interest, I learned something of what those young people felt about being Aborigines in Queensland, and I hope they were able to understand that Christianity was not just for the more privileged whites. What particular aspects of Scripture speak to us in 21st century Europe? Are there concerns and longings that the Bible can address? I believe there are. For a start there is a real concern for the environment and the future of our planet. Also, people need to know that they count, and they have real value. Love, hope and trust are not readily available in a consumer world where the "now" of things is what matters. The future can be frightening. The Christian faith has all of these to offer, and we need to ensure they are included in the "spiritual supermarket". We have to be down to Earth, but then not be shy to address the questions of the heavens.

God in Human Flesh – Recognition and Affirmation

One of the most pressing needs of young people in Europe in today's fluid culture is to know they matter, if possible ultimately, and that they have a place in life and a purpose in living. Many people today, especially young people, feel 'all at sea' – an expression that reveals the feeling of being in a fluid environment. The world takes on a completely knew look when a person feels wanted, has a role to play, or something to contribute. The trouble with our existence in a fluid state is that nothing is designed to last. An example of this is the acceptance of serial monogamy that is increasingly the norm. So many young people feel unable to make a life-long commitment in marriage, and all that they can offer their partners is the knowledge that it is working now. They cannot be sure how they will feel in the future. Society has been so fluid that although we live collective lives, we are often detached from any meaningful relationships. If someone could tell of a God who has known us from the moment we began life, and who cherishes us beyond anything we can imagine, then that would be truly good news. It would indeed be a "pearl of great value" (Matt. 13:46). This is precisely the message of the Gospel writers (Luke 1:1-4, John 20:30-31).

A fundamental element of Christianity is living in relationship with God, we in him and he in us. He recognises us as who we really are. We are loved and cherished by him, and wanted not for what we give, not anything we can do or have achieved, but simply for ourselves. This is demonstrated above all in the Christian affirmation that God was born as a human being, shared what it meant to be human, and suffered and died, abandoned, rejected and despised. (Philippians 2:5-11). If this belief is sensitively and appropriately shared with people (young or old) in our hard world it is the best news of all time. The promise is that, as one of us, Christ takes us through our own experiences of pain, loss and rejection into eternal joy (John 14:1-6). If we can overcome the desensitization caused by people who call themselves Christians, yet are really seeking to found their own "empires" – embarrassing young people in their attempts to build up their own power – then the truth of what God was doing in Christ resonates perfectly with young people seeking to succeed in a tough, competitive world. In Christ we are desired and loved and invited to love in return. In order for us to do that, we have been given complete freedom of choice, because without that freedom we become automatons incapable of receiving and giving love. Now, to be truly wanted for ourselves is a priceless commodity indeed – but it is there on offer in the "supermarket of life", in the section labelled "spirituality" on the "shelf" marked "Christian", and it is offered free of charge without obligation. Of course, there are all sorts of things that we can do as a person loved by God, but his giving of love is not conditional on us agreeing to do any of them.

In the French Alps there is a mountain ski resort with much of the accommodation further down in the valley. A free bus is provided to take people the seven miles to the beginning of the ski slopes. On arrival it is hoped that most of these people will buy a pass and join in the skiing, but there is no obligation.

Those who chose not to ski are just as welcome on the bus and no pressure is put on them to sign up for anything. Nevertheless, the very sight of so many people having a wonderful time skiing is a further invitation to join in, but there are no piste officials looking down their noses at those just taking in the view! This is the nature of God's invitation to accept his love. He wants us to respond because he loves us so much, but he does not make us do anything, or believe anything we do not choose to. We can do as much or as little as we want, and call a halt or take things more slowly at any time. This is shown in the way he came to Earth as a human being, and gave himself up for us (John 3.16), again without us doing anything in return.

The benefits of this free gift, however, do require us to take a step forward and request his love. Because we have perfect freedom then the onus is on us to respond to the invitation – just as, returning to the analogy, in order to get the full benefits of the free bus I need, first, to get on it, then hire some skis and buy a pass, and finally, learn to ski. The wonderful thing is that when we respond to God's free love, not only do we get the benefits of it, we are also recognized and called by name. We already belong in his heart, and no-one is unknown to God. We are loved from the beginning, before we are even capable of realizing it (Psalm 139).

Here is something of great worth in a fluid world where it is possible as an individual to disappear from view so easily. In the past, communities were solid and their inhabitants far less mobile. Even the cities were collections of small villages where every resident was known. Today people come and go at rapid rates and few people know who their neighbour is going to be a month, or even a week hence – indeed some people would not even recognise them if they saw them. We live in networks that are highly fluid, especially in our cities where so many young people live as students or in their first jobs, unable or unwilling to tie themselves into the housing market. Living in a postmodern world can be, and often is, very lonely. The anonymity and materialist nature of postmodern society also drives some people to religious fanaticism which, perversely, is made possible by the fluidity itself and the network system[50]. Fundamentalism is dealt with in the next chapter. But for the majority of people with an inclusive vision the message that God loves unconditionally and knows everyone by name is a powerful thing, a real joy.

God in Human Flesh – Commitment and Trust

"Commitment" and "trust" are not words that fit naturally into a postmodern world. At first sight they may appear strange in the context of a chapter dealing with the 21st century. As explained in the example above concerning the provisional nature of "marriage" or "partnership" relationships, postmodern culture refuses to be tied down. In order to preserve a life style of choice, commitment is rejected. Trust becomes difficult too, because people may change their ideas and decide to chose elsewhere. Furthermore, in the market place of life, people profiting at the expense of others is always a possibility. The current maxim runs, "Everyone should be permitted to make his/her own choices so long it does not impinge on the liberty of others to chose". In practice, however, the insecure and the unscrupulous often fail to consider the other. The first are so frightened of being left out (an understandable fear), whilst the second exploit the freedom offered by the culture, and prey on the unwary. So the knowledge of a self-giving God, who loves unconditionally and is utterly dependable and unchangeable, is further good news. Christians recognize God as omnipotent and one who does not need to exploit his creatures to sustain his power. But central to the Christian message, is the belief that God actually gives up power in order to love those whom he has created. God loved the world so much he was born in human flesh so that he might rescue human beings who suffer outside of his love. This is the theology clearly summarised in the first three chapters of St. John's Gospel for example. St. Paul expresses it this way in his letter to the Philippians:

> Let each of you look not to your own interests, but to the interests of others. Let the same mind be in you that was in Christ Jesus, who, though he was in the form of God, did not regard equality with God as something to be exploited, but emptied himself, taking the form of a slave, being born in human likeness. And being found in human form, he humbled himself and became obedient to the point of death — even death on a cross. (Philippians 2:5-8)

On the night before he died, John has Jesus say to those gathered at the Last Supper:

> No one has greater love than this, to lay down one's life for one's friends. You are my friends if you do what I command you. I do not call you servants any longer, because the servant does not know what the master is doing; but I have called you friends, because I have made known to you everything that I have heard from my Father. You did not choose me but I chose you. (John 15.13-16)

This is a remarkable depth of commitment. God in Jesus is not lording it over us as someone beyond our reach but a God who calls us friends. Friends, indeed, for whom he is willing to die. Whatever theories of atonement we wish to employ, "we believe it was for us he hung and suffered there"[51] on the cross. Such commitment, therefore, enables us to trust. No matter what we might have done or how much we or the world has changed, we can expect God to be the same tomorrow as today, and completely worthy of our trust.

The Old Testament's use of the word "rock" is significant in speaking of trust (see Psalm 18 for example). The postmodern liquid world of choice has much to commend it, but no one can spend all his or her life "all at sea". Everyone needs a dependable point of reference. When I asked a class of sixth formers studying the philosophy of religion why they chose the subject (from the A level subject choices on offer), one young person explained that they were seeking for truth, and, although the search was itself absorbing, he had a genuine hope of discovering it. Far from losing interest in the possibility of a trustworthy God that genuinely recognises, affirms and is committed to humanity by becoming one of them, young people today long to hear more. The story of the God born in human flesh is truly relevant at the beginning of the 21st century.

Trinity – Community, Love, Relationship, and Dialogue.

When I was a teenager, one of the claims of Unitarian friends was that, in truth, most people did not really believe in the Trinity. Their concept of God was as a single person. Curates used to tell each other that their vicars rarely allowed them to preach at Christmas or Easter, but they nearly always got asked to preach on Trinity Sunday because the Vicar found the doctrine difficult, or feared the curate – newly out of theological college – would accuse him of some kind of heresy. How can God possibly be three yet one at the same time? The answer we were given is that all things are possible with God. But why trinity? The truth is that in the mid twentieth century most Christians, if they were honest with themselves, never saw the point of three in one.

The legend of St. Patrick's trefoil shamrock is often quoted (three leaves yet one leaf), triangles (three sides yet one figure), water (three states – ice, liquid and steam but the same substance). All of this was, of course, recognized as inadequate. Such mathematical games do little to recommend Christianity today. But if we can shake ourselves free from Enlightenment traditional, linear thinking, I believe we have, in the Trinity, a powerful way of demonstrating (in a world that has re-discovered multi-level, non-linear reasoning) that God is not a concept that needs to disappear due to mathematical impossibility. God is not governed by Euclidean geometry any more than twenty-first century science is. We have moved on. We are free to explore expressions of God that seemed undesirable and backward looking to 19th and 20th century Christians within a modernist culture.

The New Guinea Pidgin English expression used by some missionaries to describe God to the local people was, "Bigfella man i stap long on topsaid" (The big man who lives above). Most missionaries avoided this of course, but it serves to demonstrate how reluctant some Christians of the time were to try and explain divinity very deeply. Not only is God a solid entity, he is also anthropomorphic and placed wholly outside of his creation. In British Sign Language, used by the

Deaf community, God is indicated as "up above" with the right index finger pointing directly upwards. Of course it is possible, in Pidgin and BSL as well as in English, to explain that God came in Christ and lived among us, or that God the Holy Spirit dwells within us, but we are still left, along with 99% of children (and, I suspect, many adults too) with the idea that God is "really", ordinarily, a kindly but very powerful gentleman who lives in heaven and wants to be our Father. Persons are perceived as solid – they cannot be in more than one place at a time (even if the boss expects them to be!). Father, Son and Spirit have become fixed entities, so common thinking envisages three sub-gods with different jobs within the one God. This is a heresy – but try and explain that to those not acquainted with patristics! For generations many ordinary Christians (and perhaps less ordinary ones too) have just accepted that God is "Three in One" and tried not to think about it too much. We accept that God is like that, and since he is beyond our understanding, he can be a Trinity if he wants to be. But that is to miss a huge opportunity.

The concept of the Trinity has much to tell us about God that we *can* understand, if we get away from thinking of God in solid mathematical terms. Indeed the idea of "Trinity" has a great deal that will excite those looking to grow spiritually. For a couple of centuries Christians may have been embarrassed by their inability to speak of God in modernist scientific terms, but this is no longer the case. Not only can we dare to speak of a God that "does not add up" in those terms, but we must. Science has moved on and so must we if we want people to take Christian doctrine seriously. Many young people today are engaging with philosophy of religion in their teens. So lets us "go for it" and speak of God as dynamic, fluid, all-pervading, and multidimensional as well as personal.

At a basic level, what we have in God is something that develops the simple idea that we are loved and wanted. Here, within God's own nature, is communion and love. God is self sufficient in that he does not "need" his creatures to complete himself in the way that human beings need other human beings in order to give and receive love. His self-giving is, therefore, truly selfless. Compare this with the self sacrifice of Sydney Carton, for example, in Dicken's, *A Tale of Two Cities*, where the brave man gives his life for love of a woman whom he can never possess. It is selfless in the sense that he asks nothing in return, but it is done in order to fulfil his own sense of having done something truly useful at the end of what he sees as his own, hitherto useless, life. At his death Carton ponders on the lasting esteem with which he knows he will be held by the one he loves, and all those around her. Yet God does not need our esteem or even our love. He desires them because he wants to see us complete, but he does not *need* them. God is complete community within himself. To know this is to understand that God does not seek to welcome me for any other reason than that I am; that I am truly loved, wholly and completely for myself.

But the possibility of Trinity is far richer than this. Within God himself there is movement, dynamic relationship and dialogue. Paul Fiddes is a theologian speaking in and for a postmodern world. He wants to get away from thinking of Trinity as representing three subjects, or modes of being, which relate to each other within one substance and see God as an "event of relationship" or "three movements of relationship subsisting in one event".[52] He continues:

> Of course it is not possible to visualize, paint, or etch in stone or glass three interweaving relationships, or three movements of being characterized by their relations, without subjects exercising them. But then this ought to be a positive advantage in thinking about God, who cannot be objectified like other objects in the world" (Fiddes: 36)

Such a Trinity is one we do not observe from the outside, one which we seek to describe or explain, but one in which we participate. He explains:

> Thus, through our participation, we can identify three distinct movements of speech, emotion, and action which are like relationships 'from father to son', 'from son to father' and a movement of 'deepening relations'. They are mutual relationships of ecstatic, outward-going love, giving and receiving. Actively they are such moments as originating, responding, opening; passively they are moments of being glorified, being sent, being breathed. (Fiddes: 38)

Pete Ward, reflecting on these contributions of Fiddes, sees a way forward for the Church to become more fluid within a liquid society. Trinity represents the liquid state of God enabling and leading to "liquid church":

> If God is seen as a flow of relationships among Father, Son, and Holy Spirit, Then we find here a significant boost to a more fluid kind of church. ... The vision of a church as networks of relationship and communication suddenly takes on a powerful symbolic significance in the light of these ideas. The static monolith of the congregation is replaced by a dynamic, inclusive, and fluid dance of intimate communication. In this sense liquid church does not just reflect the life of God. It joins in with that life and it is indwelt by that life: liquid God and liquid church. (Ward, 55)

We shall return to these ideas when we consider how the church can best communicate the riches of Christian spirituality at a local level.

John Atherton uses the word "dialogic" to describe the Trinity. Today "we are led deeper into a Trinitarian God in ways which connect powerfully and decisively with what Christian discipleship and human living will need to become if we are to overcome the great global challenges." He continues:

> It takes us into a God who is source of all form yet formless; source of thought yet beyond thought. It becomes glimpse of the timeless wholeness of all reality, the wisdom of God 'before' the creation of the world, into which we can now begin to enter. It is a journey through the rich multiplicity of the created order of the environment into an immeasurably rich multiplicity of God. (Atherton, 6)

Here are words such as "form – formless", "journey" and "multiplicity" all of which resonate with postmodern thinking. Atherton describes the nature of God as "dialogic". This world is one of "increasing plurality" with "unifying demands". There is no way forward except through "partnership and reconciliation" (Atherton, 7). He sees four aspects of a dialogic God that speak directly to the world of today.

First, "a God in dialogue with itself, and therefore with the Other, points to the transcendent dimension of existence" (Atherton, 8). In recent decades much emphasis has been laid on the immanence of God to compensate for the earlier emphasis on a God who is Lord, King and Master. Such a concept fits a hierarchical society in which human authority had to be maintained. But recent and welcome moves to recognise the pastoral nature of leadership reflects a picture of the God who lives within and alongside, the Friend which we have referred to above. This has led to a diminution of emphasis on the transcendent. But there is among many young people today a new longing to reach outward and seek the "Other".

This is seen in the great interest in the science of cosmology, and the search for the Theory of Everything (TOE). This search for answers to the meaning of the universe reveals itself in science fiction too, where the truth that the "search" is just as important as the answer – although it would be nice to think that one day (even if not here on earth) answers will be given. Douglas Adams, for example, in his 1970s radio series, *The Hitchhiker's Guide to the Galaxy,* has an ultra-powerful computer that comes up with the answer to the "meaning of everything" as being "42". Now the travellers have to find the question that prompts the answer, and this the computer cannot provide. In the television version, as the tale ends with the seekers walking away defeated, a primitive man discovers the question as he scratches away on a stone. The question to which the answer is "42" turns out to be "6 x 9"! This encapsulates the postmodern dilemma, which in its own way is delightfully appealing. We should not, therefore, be surprised at the interest there is in Trinity. It has an appeal to today's generation in its attempts to reach out (or into) the ultimate "Other".

The second aspect of a dialogic God, Atherton explains, is about "learning from encounters with others" (Atherton, 8). Listening to what others have to contribute is to reflect the nature of God. Atherton speaks of F. D. Maurice who was, "a 'digger' into deeper truths through the recognition of the limitations of tradition revealed through engagement with other traditions." (Atherton, 8). This is not to live in a world so fluid that we can either say nothing at all, or a complete *Via Negativa*[53] that leads us to abandon any Christian affirmation of faith, but a preparedness to listen, and enhance our relationship with God as we move in partnership alongside them. If the Christian concept of the Trinity incorporates such dialogue then this is not only going to enrich our understanding of the world and the knowledge of how other traditions understand it, it is also going to enable us to understand the value of our own inherited Christian understandings and traditions and how they are relevant in present times. It is this insight that gives rise to theology that takes account of the world as it is, and not just how we think it ought to be.

Thirdly, says Atherton, a dialogic God, "provokes and fosters the development of Christian character through particular virtues". Christianity, he writes, "can be expressed as an ethic of unequivocal neighbourliness, of the recognition of the Other as neighbour, as Good Samaritan" (Atherton, 9). Engaging with the world's needs springs from the depth of the relationship of God within himself. We develop a reciprocity with others, an ability to feel what it is like to be them. We are led to, "enact the generosity of God, which does not claim reciprocal rights, but gives without counting the cost ...". This has always been a major element in Christianity springing from the life and example of Christ himself and summed up in the judgement parable of the sheep and the goats (Matthew 25.31-46). Christian neighbourliness, springing from the very nature of God, neither discriminates nor holds back in giving. "If then there is any encouragement in Christ, any consolation from love, any sharing in the Spirit, any compassion and sympathy, make my joy complete: be of the same mind, having the same love, being in full accord and of one mind", declares St. Paul (Philippians 2.1-2). Sometimes we are tempted to put our Christian concern into a separate compartment and call it "The Department for Social Responsibility" or "Church and Society" or some such title. In doing so we run the risk of believing that there can be a sort of Christianity that does *not* relate to the world. The nature of "church" and its relationship with "society" will be discussed in greater length later, but it is important to see here how the way we respond to our neighbours derives directly from the nature of trinitarian, dialogic God, itself. She or he who is "in God" cannot be separate from her or his neighbour at any time. The nature of God is fellowship and as such leads us into complete identification with others. It is the generosity within a dialogic God, as Atherton says, "that has, in the end, to inspire Jubilee 2000's campaign on international debt, and the altruistic nature of its claims." (Atherton, 10)

Finally, observes Atherton, "facing great global challenges requires dialogue between the great faiths", and a dialogic God not only permits full participation, it requires it, but it is not the kind of dialogue that seeks to produce a hybrid form of religion that denies the integrity or traditions of the different faiths. Atherton concludes:

> The task is to be secure enough in one's personal and communal identity to be able to reach out to the Other without feeling unduly threatened. Yet equally that reaching out cannot be so extended as to become lost in the Other. Losing difference in such a way contradicts the different Persons in the dialogic God. The human path is likewise about preserving and promoting similarities and differences, including processes of global integration and fragmentation. (Atherton, 11)

In this process, Christians should hold on to their own traditional beliefs, including the doctrine of the incarnation, and the divinity of Christ, as well as the Trinity. In the world of today, people are not seeking a watered down faith in order to make it more palatable. They want to encounter spiritualities in all the richness of their scriptures, traditions and histories. To bring that to a postmodern world is to respect it and in so doing gain respect. What we must not do is fail to listen, honestly and carefully, in return. When we are closed we raise suspicion and mistrust, and deny the truth that is encompassed in the Trinity, a dynamic, dialogic God in which we live and grow.

René Descartes (1596-1650), a founding father of the Enlightenment, in declaring, "I think, therefore I am" perceived human beings as ultimately separate individuals. Paul Fiddes and others today advocate, "I relate, therefore I am". We are who we are because of our relationships and we know ourselves through them too. God is who God is through his being an "event of relationships" and so in God we participate in a relationship that gives us complete reality, ultimate significance in, through and beyond time and space.

So the concept of Trinity does not jar the postmodern mentality as it did the modern, nor do postmodern seekers in spirituality have to be experts in theology or church history to grasp the significance of a God who is Three and One for the world today. To be able to speak of participating in God who is an "event of relationship" is to meet our young people, full of exploratory zeal, with an idea of God that begs to be "encountered". It embraces all freedoms of a fluid, postmodern world and reveals the emptiness of the world of total illusion referred to by Jean

Baudrillard and others.

Creation, The Garden of Eden and The Kingdom of God.

As we explore the depths of God, however, we do not become disembodied or other worldly. Everything is connected to God who in-dwells not only the spiritual but the physical too. The "Event" that is God is both immanent and transcendent. Theologians often refer us to Gerard Manly Hopkins' poem, *God's Grandeur*[54] in which God's grandeur is not overcome by the exploitation of creation by nineteenth century industry and grime. He is not detached from the world in some sort of spiritual haven. Today's young people insist that we keep the health of the planet in focus as we explore the things of the spirit. In their minds they are intimately connected:

> ... Generations have trod, have trod, have trod;
> And all is seared with trade; bleared, smeared with toil;
> And wears man's smudge and shares man's smell: the soil
> Is bare now, nor can foot feel, being shod.
> And for all this, nature is never spent;
> There lives the dearest freshness deep down things;
> And through the last lights off the black West went
> Oh, morning, at the brown brink eastward, springs -
> Because the Holy Ghost over the bent
> World broods with warm breast and with ah! bright wings.

The advancement of science in the last three hundred years has enabled humanity to exploit our planet's resources at a rate not conceived of by those who lived only a few generations ago. More recently, science has also provided the means to monitor this exploitation, and to warn us of the consequences of continuing as we are. As we discovered before, the general public does not know whom to trust, if anyone. Big business and politics are always suspected of seeking profit or power (or both), and much of the science is sponsored by those who seek to gain advantages for their own causes. What was once thought of as a cynical attitude is now regarded as, perhaps, a realistic one. But enough has been said to alarm the general public in Europe and give increasing concern for the fragility of the environment. Some have changed their life-styles – not an easy thing to do whilst many around them are determined in their short-term materialism. The young are the most idealistic and their attitudes should be both commended and encouraged. They seek to be "green" in their approach to living. More and more people try to recycle their waste, buy organically produced food and insulate their homes. They are conscious of their responsibility for our planet and seek to find their proper place in it. They recognise that they do not stand apart from the rest of creation, and (except for a few Creationists) understand that we are a product of evolution along with all that has life. Has not Christianity got something profound to contribute here? Does not this development reflect something of God's relationship with his creation?

The doctrine of creation that emerges from a critical understanding of Scripture, reflects humanity's relationship with the Creator and his creation. First, it marvels in the greatness and goodness of God, and then reflects on the way we should care for things, including each other.

In Psalm 8 we have this hymn of praise:

> When I look at your heavens, the work of your fingers,
> the moon and the stars that you have established;
> what are human beings that you are mindful of them,
> mortals that you care for them?
> Yet you have made them a little lower than God,
> and crowned them with glory and honour.
> You have given them dominion over the works of your hands;
> you have put all things under their feet,
> all sheep and oxen,
> and also the beasts of the field,
> the birds of the air, and the fish of the sea,
> whatever passes along the paths of the seas.
> O LORD, our Sovereign,
> how majestic is your name in all the earth.

The accounts of creation in Genesis (Genesis 1 – 2.4a and Genesis 2.4b – 3.13) also emphasise, not only the goodness of God and creation, but humanity's responsibility regarding it.

In recent years a number of books have been written on this subject, mainly directed at the Church, to help it take account of "green" concerns.[55] But, as we have noted before, politicians and big business have been resolute at ignoring the questions. The most Christian of nations (in terms of the proportion of people attending church), the United States of America, has a very poor record in this regard. This does not help young people in a world of choice to be attracted towards the Christian offerings here. Yet, the theologies of creation, if truly heard, make a meaningful spiritual contribution to the current culture. Perhaps we ought to stack them, not just on the shelf marked "Christian", but also on the shelf marked "Earth spirituality", alongside New Age ideas and neo-paganism, for surely Christianity has a depth of understanding to compete in this department.

Christianity has grown up for centuries in touch with the countryside of Europe. Its festivals reflect the European seasons and in some cases grew out of the pagan festivals that preceded them. It is not only the occasions of Rogationtide and Harvest, but Christmas is timed to coincide with the pagan celebration of the winter solstice. Easter, with its symbol of the Easter egg, is associated with the new life of the Spring. In the northern hemisphere, we often take this for granted so deeply has it become part of the culture. Whilst it may be possible in some ways to ignore the changing of the seasons in our towns and cities it is not so possible in the countryside and here traditional Christianity retains some of its appeal. Nevertheless, even here, the postmodern world is having its way. The village shop and post-office are disappearing as more and more people take to their cars to visit the supermarkets in the country towns. People expect the freedom to choose, and villagers born and bred in the local countryside are an increasing rarity. Young people move out, attracted by the choices provided by urban areas, (or are driven out by lack of work opportunities or the high price of housing caused by the numbers of older suburban dwellers moving into a rural idyll in their retirement, or simply buying week-end cottages). But in the midst of all this the environment is a place where important choices have to be made and in which Christianity has much to contribute – if and when its offerings are on view.

It is not just the environment but its people that concern us in today's world. Millions of Europeans show disquiet over "third world" poverty and exploitation as demonstrated in the recent Jubilee 2000 campaign for the cancelling of third world debt. The methods and lasting effects of the use of war has raised much anxiety in recent years, especially over Iraq; a question that has divided Europe politically, but which has brought to light a developing opposition to war as a method of solving problems.

The Bible advances an explanation for the breakdown of human relations and their consequences and explains how God might deal with the situation. Leaving aside, for the moment, the need to understand how the bible came to be and how to interpret it today, the story of the Garden of Eden (Genesis 2 and 3) and that of Cain and Abel (Genesis 4.1-16) give expression to the way humanity is seen to behave in the world. Here we see greed, exploitation, dishonesty, beguiling of the innocent, shame, guilt, exclusion, jealousy, deceit, violence and cover up. When Cain answers God's question as to the whereabouts of his brother with the words, "I do not know; am I my brother's keeper?" (Genesis 4.9) he is speaking directly to a debate that is raging in our contemporary world. How much are we responsible for others, especially those who, due to the world's inequalities, are unable to visit the postmodern "supermarket" of opportunity. We may live in a world that allows people to chose, but in practice many, especially in the third world, have no freedom at all. What concerns them is where they are going to find their next meal, or how they are going to cope when their parents die young of AIDS. Christian faith has powerful things to say in response to this question – not least because the God who gave his all for his friends makes it abundantly clear that this is the way he wants us to behave to one another too. "For I have set you an example, that you also should do as I have done to you."(John 13.15), he says at the Last Supper. For those who participate in God, there is not only the example but the strength given to fulfil it. "Keep on doing the things that you have learned and received and heard and seen in me, and the God of peace will be with you." (Philippians 4.9) promises Paul. To the Corinthians, engaged in a battle with the things of the world, he writes: "So if anyone is in Christ, there is a new creation: everything old has passed away; see, everything has become new! All this is from God, who reconciled us to himself through Christ, and has given us the ministry of reconciliation" (2 Corinthians 5.17).

Popular concern is not just for the environment but also for those who miss out so much through poverty brought on by human injustice, exploitation, ignorance and conflict. Christianity has been involved in such concern from Jesus, himself. His first appearance in the synagogue in Nazareth for example sets the scene for his whole ministry. He quotes from Isaiah: "The Spirit of the Lord is upon me, because he has anointed me to bring good news to the poor. He has sent me to proclaim release to the captives and recovery of sight to the blind, to let the oppressed go free, to proclaim the year of the Lord's favour." (Luke 4:18-19). In the nineteenth century this became properly organized in Britain. The Salvation Army[56] and the Church Army[57], for example, were set up by Christians not only to do the work but to remind the rest of the church of its responsibility. One speaker, outlining the history of the Children's Society (which began life as the Church of England homes for "Waifs and Strays"[58]) spoke of a point when, as well as helping homeless children they began asking why they were homeless. "As well as fishing children out of the (metaphorical) river", he said, "we began asking how they were falling into it, and we looked to see if prevention was not possible."[59] They thus became involved in political dialogue. Politicians have either welcomed such Christian "action" or hated it. Many have wished Christians would confine themselves to the "spiritual" realm and leave the "secular politics" up to them. Even before it was published, in December 1985 Norman Tebbit and other government ministers denounced the Church of England's publication *Faith in the City* describing it as Marxist.[60] Yet neither *Faith in the City* nor its counterpart *Faith in the Countryside* (1991) were based on political doctrine, but on properly researched theology of God's relationship with his creation and with his people.

Christians ought not to separate their faith from social and environmental policy, and should be deeply involved in issues of poverty, justice, peace and prosperity. Christian Aid works under the slogan, "We believe in life before death"[61], affirming that Christians are interested in this world as well as the next.

Young people have, perhaps, more interest in the fate of the planet than in what happens beyond it – they have only just begun to explore life and want to enjoy it and contribute something to it. If Christianity is to seem at all relevant to them it must not only have something to say about human life and its potential, but be seen to be active at all levels of the church. Our departments of social responsibility remind us that Christianity, and the God it proclaims, is about changing the world because he made and loves it.

The stories of Creation, the Garden of Eden and the life-giving spirit that God promises to address the problems of the world, square with our culture today. The question that follows is: How can we present them so that they can be discovered by the many who never darken the doors of our churches? But before we go on to seek answers to this question, there is still another exciting Christian contribution that we need to explore.

Glory, Resurrection, Hope and Baptism

The things of this world are important for young people but there is still a longing to encounter that which is beyond, that which has eternal significance. Spiritual experience is very much "in vogue" and is no longer thought of as second class or mere superstition. The numinous and the mysterious appeal to young people. Poetry, art, music are popular. Galleries and concert halls are well patronised. Silent retreats have experienced something of a revival of late and many young people seek time just to "chill" – take a step back from the rush of everyday life and reflect. We should not, therefore, be afraid of speaking of the glory and otherness of God, and our Christian journey into a daunting, awesome, and even dangerous, divine presence.

The concept of resurrection, for example, like Trinity, is something that has become more readily acceptable today than in the Modern world of the first half of the 20th century. In a logical, scientific world spiritual things fail to fit in. Miracles and the like could all be explained, or if they could not (as, say, in the New Testament) the account of them was deemed to be flawed or embellished. The humanity of Christ was an easier concept to understand than his divinity. Jesus' relationships and faith could be thought of in psychological terms. His life and death could be seen in the context of the politics of the day. But in this modernist world his resurrection did not fit in, it was something that belied ordinary experience. All sorts of psychological reasons could be advanced for why the disciples believed he had risen, but the simple explanation required a leap out of the world of science.

But in a postmodern world things have changed. Why should God be a slave to the laws of physics? In any case, the more scientists investigate, the more they find to change what we had previously believed about nature. Science, like other things in a postmodern world, has a sense of provisionality about it and has lost the solidity with which it was once endowed. As we have seen, a hundred years ago the laws of Euclidean geometry and Newtonian physics were believed to be applicable throughout the universe. Today we speak of time warps, folded space, and string theories. This is not science-fiction. Science fiction itself has moved from journeys to Mars to multi-level consciousness and explorations into philosophical concepts. Films like the *The Matrix* are reminiscent of Plato's cave – (Plato himself is being studied by many sixteen year olds in Britain with enthusiasm)[62].

So the idea of an after-life does not appear so much unscientific wishful thinking as it might have been for those living before the 1960s. It is still, of course, faith dependent – but the step of faith is not so much against the run of things. A person does not have to think in different compartments as they once did. Scientists do not have to keep spiritual thinking "separate" from their working lives. Young thinking people need not keep their thoughts so private because, not only does society allow them the privilege to do their "own thing", but also admits to thinking about life in different dimensions. Serial existence, or re-incarnation, for example, is amazingly popular. Human resurrection is, therefore, something that will be taken seriously among young people today. And, of course, it offers much more than other theories of everlasting life or re-incarnation. If people are taking ideas from Eastern religions seriously, why not those of Christianity?

Resurrection in the Christian story contains all the hope of recognition, affirmation, love and meaning, and extends them beyond this world. Resurrection contains the promise of continued identity and continued relationships. It also speaks of something better than this world – "he will wipe every tear from their eyes. Death will be no more; mourning and crying and pain will be no more." (Revelation 21.4). In a transient existence resurrection contains the hope of continued exploration together with a development of personality begun on Earth. In the words of St. Paul: "So we do not lose heart. Even though our outer nature is wasting away, our inner nature is being renewed day by day. For this slight momentary affliction is preparing us for an eternal weight of glory beyond all measure, because we look not at what can be seen but at what cannot be seen; for what can be seen is temporary, but what cannot be seen is eternal." (2 Corinthians 4.16-18).

But among ordinary people in recent times resurrection has been misunderstood. It is commonly confused with simple resuscitation – the sort of thing that is expressed in Henry Scott Holland's phrase, "I have just moved into the next room"[63]. Whilst that may express the idea of continuity the idea of resurrection goes far beyond that. It involves re-creation at a level and degree that is not possible without death. This is expressed more clearly in the well known chorus, *Spirit of the Living God.*[64] "Spirit of the Living God, fall afresh on me, break me, melt me, mould me, fill me". To be really effective the process requires breaking to the point of death. This is prefigured in the symbolism of baptism. In baptism we transfer from dependence on the world to dependence on God. We no longer rely on the things that are transient but live the life that God gives – a life which is eternal. (In New Testament Greek terms, we move from "*bios*" to "*zoe*".) The "prayer over the water" in the *Common Worship* baptism service runs: "We thank you, almighty God, for the water of baptism. In it we are buried with Christ in his death. By it we share in his resurrection. Through it we are reborn by the Holy Spirit."[65] There is not, and ought not to be, something cosy and gentle about baptism. In the past I believe the church has either colluded in the social traditions or superstitions that have surrounded a right of passage for babies, or has been uncaring in demanding people demonstrate their sincerity by some form of church-going. (Baptism is about living the "Jesus way" – not about forcing people to attend services they find either difficult to get to or difficult to understand, or, as is more often the case, both.) However, in the twenty-first century we should certainly not turn folk away who come with their babies, or as is increasingly happening, asking for baptism for themselves. We live in an age when to seek a christening nearly always has a religious motive, no matter how hidden or secondary. Young parents rarely have their child 'done' these days just to please older generations. At one time some grandparents refused to allow them into the house until the right had been performed. Most parents today want a "spiritual blessing" for the child, even though that might be weak or misunderstood. In my experience they are often ready to listen to deeper theology and richer meaning. They are not afraid to talk about difficult concepts, and are not generally embarrassed by "God talk". Once ultimate questions are being addressed it is amazing just how often the questions flow. Young people want to talk about life, death, the universe and the meaning of everything! The demands that ministers and congregations become more deeply informed about their faith, and being prepared to become involved in on-going contact with young families. who find Sunday worship difficult for a number of reasons. Young people want us to be prepared to speak profoundly, and with sensitivity and in ways they can understand, not dumbing down the wonder of God and the depth of his relationship with his creation. They want us to explain the full richness of resurrection and eternal life and the force of what it means to say, in the words of the baptism promises, "I turn to Christ". So long as we do not become fervent or declamatory (a big turn off), and are sensitive and caring, we will be welcomed as authentic witnesses to God's good news in Jesus. We will be valued channels of the story of hope. The concepts of resurrection, hope and eternal glory are not only wholly welcome in an uncertain, fluid society, they are also longed for.

In this chapter we have looked at some of the most important aspects of the Christian faith that have real meaning in today's world. There are others, but sufficient has been said to indicate that the Christian Gospel can be perceived as both relevant and desirable by those thoroughly steeped in the culture of choice. The challenge is to see how these Christian offerings can be heard and understood. This is the challenge we shall attempt to address in the chapters that follow.

6. The Problems of Living and Believing in a Fluid World

In order for young people to respond to the things Christianity has to offer they need to hear them and see them in action. In this chapter we shall explore the problems Christians are facing in passing on their Gospel. Quite clearly it is young people more than any other group that are failing to connect with the churches as they find them today. Why should this be?

Imagine being in a foreign country with which you are not familiar, and wanting to buy basic necessities. In 21st century Europe, it is most likely that you would go to a supermarket. Even though you may not speak the language you could find most of your needs by scanning the shelves without having to ask for anything. However, if there were no supermarket, or if what you needed was only to be found in a specific shop with a counter behind which stood a shopkeeper – even with the friendliest smile, some people would be diffident about going in. The products may look strange, and you don't know their names. You may not be aware of the price, or be familiar with the money. If you were, perhaps, driven by hunger, you may attempt to buy, but could end up with something you did not really want, or wonder whether you had been taken advantage of. However, no matter how kind and honest the shopkeeper, the experience may still be off-putting. If the product you wanted was something you did not absolutely need, you may well decide to walk by – unless you were an outgoing adventurous kind of person – and not all are!

Working from this story, imagine what it is going to be like for a young person in the market for some spiritual fulfilment. They may be aware of a real hunger, but where are they to begin and whom can they trust? For the most part the Gospel is so very inaccessible to the person who just wants to see what it's about. It is difficult to gain more than book knowledge of what Christianity is, without getting involved.

Church Buildings

Sometimes it comes in old, often unwelcoming buildings, huge numbers of which are kept locked except at times of services. When they are open, say in tourist areas, it is astonishing how often they are visited by the general public who just want to come and look. There is, of course, an interest in history or beautiful architecture, but there is also an interest in the Christianity that has given rise to it. As people walk round, so they look at the bookstalls and not infrequently buy from them, or help themselves to free literature. But even these places can become scary when services begin. Most cathedrals for example, exclude the public from wandering around near to where a service is taking place behind a forbidding rope with a notice "Service in Progress". Of course, access to the service is free and welcomed (and that's not always obvious) – but once you go beyond the rope you feel you are expected to look intelligent, at least in some small way. That can be really frightening. The whole thing seems to be something for the initiated. Young people may ask themselves, "Do they really want me here,? Am I gate crashing?" One imagines that all those others there know exactly what to do, and the newcomer feels as awkward as a person in a foreign country who does not know the language. Not knowing what's going to happen, or how you should behave, or whether you ought to be there, or if you will like what's going to happen, or even whether it is safe, can be a terrifying or embarrassing experience. Now this may sound odd to some older readers who have grown up with going to church or Sunday School. "Safe! Of course its safe!" But they know the culture and the form of worship, and what to expect. Those who are not familiar with a service do feel they stand out; if you doubt it just look at their faces. If older readers want to get a feeling for it imagine yourself going into a night club in a city centre. Do you think you could get in there without standing out? Would you know how to behave? Would you appreciate the music? What would you do if someone asked you to dance? What would you do if no-one asked you to dance? It's exactly the same feeling for young people not brought up to attend church – they feel totally out of place.

Today vast numbers of young people have never been into a church at all. In the parish in which I live the church is always open during daylight hours. The tower, however, has to be kept locked for safety reasons but one summer it was thought a good idea to open it every Thursday in August for tourists to view the town from the top. This was combined with a conducted tour of the church building, and an invitation to tea in the church hall next door. To our surprise (or perhaps we should not have been surprised at all) over half the people that took advantage of the tour were local people. One man in his forties admitted that he had never been into the church although he had lived all his life within a quarter of a mile of it. He had wanted to look in for years but had never done so. He knew it was kept open but had never felt he could "just wander in like that". His story is not that unusual. How could anyone be in trouble by visiting a church that is clearly open to the public? The congregation of that same church wanted local children to feel the church building belonged to them and they were invited just to call and look around, or pray there, whenever they wished. Two little girls took this invitation to heart and decided to visit the church sometime after school. The person whose job it was to lock up that day always checked that there was no-one in the building before he locked it, but the sight of a large strange man frightened the little girls who hid from him behind a pew and they were locked in. Fortunately there was a person tending to the gardens just outside the door who heard crying from inside. She ran off to get the key, and when the door was eventually opened the two girls shot out and disappeared never to be seen again! One can only guess what they told their class-mates. Imagine being shut in there, in the evening gloom, with those ghostly statues – and in the middle of a spooky churchyard too! Church buildings, with all their advantages are not always the best places to advertise the "Good News".

The Generation Gap

One of the other difficulties of presenting Christianity through churches is the "generation gap". Many church congregations these days consist of people in the latter half of their lives. Young people are becoming increasingly rare in regular church services. One church we visited could claim up to forty members of the ages of 16 to 18 years in their youth club. They were widely acclaimed as the most successful church in the diocese for work with young people. By contrast, parishes with more than forty old people are very common indeed. The very fact that church members are on the old side, makes it very hard for young people to feel they can join in. Even if they have been brought up to understand church so that they have no fear of it, they find it unappealing. Who can blame them? Young people want to be with young people and feel out of place, bored or sometimes (but not always) unwanted among older people. Whatever the appeal of the ideas of God, church is not meeting their own needs of community and fellowship. Older people interested in sharing faith with young people have to overcome huge divisions caused by the prejudice, fear and sheer lack of communication we have noted in chapter four.

Therefore, if churches at both national and local level are going to be effective communicators of the Good News of Jesus Christ, which has so much to contribute in a postmodern society, they must be fully aware of the problems produced by the generation gap. Ministers, priests and congregations will have to be strongly aware of the danger of appearing (if not actually being) judgemental. They will also have to try and understand something of the pressures young people are under and what it is like to be young *now* (not what it was like to be young in the past). Then they must make the moves that impress upon young people that they genuinely care. All of this is a tall order and hard work – but if we are serious about passing on the Good News of Jesus, not one we can shirk.

The Package Deal

Another problem is that Christianity often comes as a package deal. There is nothing wrong with package deals in themselves, sometimes they suit the need. For example, if I wanted to buy a set of replacement bulbs for a new car I would be delighted to find a complete set, neatly packaged with a bulb for every possible eventuality. But if I were interested in just one specific bulb then I would not be interested in the complete package. If a particular shop did not sell single bulbs, I might very well leave that shop in search of one that did. This is both the advantage and disadvantage of courses. Programmes such as the *Alpha Course* or *Emmaus Course,*[66] for example have done an amazing work in helping young people in particular to an understanding of Christianity that has given them a very real entry into the things of God, and many have much to be grateful for because of them. However, they do demand a degree of commitment and some knowledge to start with. For a great many of the participants on these courses it is not their first encounter with Christianity. Others have friends with them whom they have learned to trust whom they believe will look after them or allow them the freedom to withdraw if they choose. These courses are package deals. You have to begin where they begin, and they are designed to introduce people into regular church worship and membership. Inquirers may wish to seek God, not the Church, but the way things are presented they cannot have one without the other. Courses mostly do not meet the need of a postmodern seeker wanting to find out about just one of the teachings of Christianity, such as those described in chapter five.

Proponents of the course may explain that you cannot just pick the bits of Christianity that appeal and leave the rest – the Christian faith is more than a series of separate ideas. That is true, but the question at issue here is how people discover and own the things they believe. Returning to my analogy regarding the bulbs for my new car, it might be highly advisable to buy the whole set, and the assistant in the motor accessory shop might suggest it, but if I were not ready in my own mind to invest in this way he would be a wise assistant to find the one bulb I required. Whether or not he agreed with the customer he would apply the maxim, "The customer is always right". Note the language here too – shop employees are called "assistants" because the emphasise is on helping the customer make his or her own purchases. Courses have their place, and we do need them, especially if they are geared to help people to live in our time, but we should be aware that, used inappropriately, they can be a turn-off. It is vital that Christians listen carefully to what inquirers are asking and assist them on their personal journey. Whether we approve of it or not we live in a postmodern age in which young people feel, naturally, that they have the right to pick and choose. We need to recognise that and work with it.

Courses or none, we should be more aware of the tendency to confuse being "Christ" centred with being "Church" centred. In some places there appears little, if any, distinction between applying for membership of the Church and seeking the Kingdom of God. We should endeavour to discover ways in which people can learn about Christianity without having to "join up" first. The "package deal" may appeal to people wanting to increase numbers in their churches, but it doesn't necessarily appeal to those just wanting to know about Jesus Christ.

Organized Church

Churches of all denominations are organized into some kind of structure, including those who reject the old hierarchies of bishops and priests in favour of local leadership. There are membership lists, electoral rolls, stewardship schemes, church councils, elders or churchwardens. There is always a leader or leadership team in which some kind of authority is vested. But in a postmodern world authorities of any kind, including religious ones, are not fashionable; they hark back to a society without choice or adventure. In seeking to guide and advise, they can also seek to deprive people of the liberty to chose. Here, the tensions between the traditional way the churches have been organized and that which is being forced on it by the reduction in the numbers of local clergy and ministers have been under way for at least three decades. But it is not just the reduction in the number of clergy that give rise to the strains. Local clergy and ministers are aware of a deepening cultural gulf among the people they serve. As we have previously observed, those of older generations live in a different world from those aged 50 or less. This rift in the way people look at the world, the fundamentally different basic, often unspoken, cultural assumptions, creates an enormous tension within local communities, especially where there is a large proportion of older people. The church is, as we have seen, largely made up of congregations of older people whose expectations of a dwindling number of clergy have not changed. Many of them battle to retain the model with which they grew up in the first half of the 20th century. They fight for a priest to keep the show going even though they know they cannot all succeed, and that it probably cannot last. They employ every tactic they can think of, fair and sometimes foul too, to maintain the structures they feel at home with, that which is "normal" for them. I have heard many times, expressed in resigned tones, something along the lines of: "If we manage to get a new priest I expect he will probably see me out, and then it will be someone else's problem." Sadly this narrow and selfish attitude, even if it is not intended to be, is forgetting the job of passing on the Gospel. Yet even if they do get a new minister that person is under enormous pressure to relate to a postmodern world which many of those who grew up in the 1960s and before see as the norm.

Whilst residents of a fluid society might be attracted to some of the things traditional churches offer, they are often suspicious of becoming imprisoned in an established, inflexible structure. Much Christian good news comes attached to organized church in this way and is the reason why it is rejected by so many, especially the young. One brave sixth former told me straight, "God's 'in', OK, but church is 'out'!" If we had the courage and imagination to offer our Christian doctrines, and let people take what they wish without obligation; without having to abandon their freedom to think, debate or question, then God's love would be infinitely more accessible. Indeed that is the way God actually treats his people. He offers himself freely, unconditionally without any pressure being applied (as in my example of the free bus in the previous chapter), but many of those who are already followers of the Way of Christ and who are church members find that hard to take. It is the institution that demands obedience because it is the institution that seeks to control. I am reminded of the church leader who was indignant that a young person who had belonged to his church had started attending another church in the parish with her friend. "Sheep stealing", he called it. Fortunately I met a French Catholic priest that same week who had come with a party of people on a twinning trip. When I asked him what they were going to do about joining in with Anglican worship he responded, *"Il est un Dieu, quel est le problème?"* What indeed? The trouble is that traditional church leaders tend to count their success in terms of membership. Is it not the Kingdom of God that we should be concerned with rather than impressing others with our "success"? Among some you can hear them speak of the credits awarded to each congregation – with more points being given for having young people at services. It's especially important to have them all on parade when the bishop comes![67]

Before any part of the structure can be changed it must be agreed upon in the way that the constitution provides after due and "proper" consideration of its members properly listed. Here is a world of meetings called with the right amount of notice, elected representatives, quorums, and procedures. These structures at higher levels often employ legal secretaries and the like. Now, no-one wants to object to things being done carefully, thoughtfully and prayerfully, and some of this is going to be needed to support the actual work of the Church. The trouble is that some confuse this enabling service with the real purpose of the Church. The problems occur when the structures become self-serving and the vision of what God intends for the people of God is forgotten in all the busy-ness. Indeed "busy-ness" may well become "business" because the management of the Church often reflects the nature of business corporations.

Another problem with this kind of institution is its propensity to being malevolently infiltrated. In the case of the Church it has been penetrated by those with false motives for centuries. Princes have used it for their own ends politically, and many a cleric has exploited the church for worldly gain. The scandalous appropriation of positions of power (often with money attached) in the Middle Ages and beyond was blatant.[68] Today, there is not so much money to be had, but we still have our power struggles and interest groups who manipulate to get their own way. These may not be at all subtle but, since they know how to play the system, they gain power within the institution by using its rules. All of this just adds to the lack of trust that comes with living in an age of suspicion and harms the work being done by Christians despite the structures.

The difficulty with the way the church is organized means that its members find themselves serving the institution as well as God. With the best will in the world clergy find themselves in some sort of career structure, which may not be as intense as other institutions (actual supermarkets for example) but in which they feel they need to make a good impression. The account books have to balance and it is vital that the institution raises the necessary finance. Membership and finance are linked and it becomes a "business", a religious enterprise in which membership numbers are vital. A great deal of time and effort is employed in maintaining the structures. Those who resist this are caught in a "catch 22" situation. A bishop once inquired whether our parish had anyone capable of being involved in a diocesan working party. There were such people, I replied, but it would be a pity to take them away from the voluntary work they were doing in the community, because people with a vision of the Kingdom were not easily found. He replied that if the diocesan working parties did not have people with such vision then things would not change. If such people were not found then the volunteers would be from among those who were committed primarily to sustaining the institution as a self-serving club. He was right, but the people who knew what was needed to proclaim the Gospel wanted to be directly engaged in it rather than debating it. They live outside the "club".

There is a way of looking at the Church which is similar to a walled garden. Inside all is kept very beautiful; the beds are weed free, the plants given proper nourishment, the flowers arranged according to colour and size, lawns kept in trim, the trees pruned and cultivated in their proper seasons to produce good wholesome fruit, and water features are kept clean and sparkling. There is, however, a door – just one – in the garden wall that is kept by God. This door is Christ. All who would aspire to come into the garden are welcome – but once in they should realize that they are "committed" – coming and going is very much looked down upon. People enter the garden by accepting Christ as their Lord and Master. The password into the garden, which is freely known because all are invited, is, "Jesus is Lord" – but it must be truly meant with heart and mind, soul and strength. Anyone seeking to come into the garden on false pretences will be sent away, or else the garden will be spoiled. Inside the garden there are gardeners (called "ministers") who ensure that things are as they should be and gently point out to people when they are failing in the duties of the residents. Those who fail are said to commit "sins". But the really terrible state of "sin" lies outside of the garden among those who have not yet sought to come in, or who have rejected the invitation. But the Lord of the Garden is compassionate and longs to have everyone he has called inside – are there not many unfilled places? So the residents of this garden are bidden to go out "into the world" and bring others in. The residents seek out those who demonstrate the most courage and possess the gift of persuasion and send them out with their blessing. They are strengthened by the knowledge that their homeland is truly inside the garden and, although they go out as "sheep among wolves", God will protect them.

Telling it like this may sound, perhaps, something of a parody, but this is how it seems to many people on the outside of organized church. Christianity can look like a club of like minded people who have separated themselves off from everyone else, who think they are better than other people, and who claim exclusive ownership of God. We need to find a model of church that is centred on the Kingdom of God, where God reigns beyond the confines of the Church. Where you find God, said Jesus, is among the hungry, thirsty, sick and imprisoned.[69]

Margaret Kane addresses this question in her book, *What Kind of God,* about being church in the north-east of England in 1986. She is frustrated in her attempts to convey to the structured church she encountered the real significance of mission and the resources and commitment she realised it needed.

> Instead of the Church questioning the world's assumption about itself and posing to it the question of God, it is the world that today questions the church about the authenticity of the God it proclaims. A remote, all-powerful, impassive God cannot answer the world's needs. A soft, indulgent God who takes no account of injustice will not suffice. Only a God who suffers in the sufferings of humanity can save. That is the God I meet in the world, find with me in whatever knocks I myself take, and recognize in Jesus Christ and in the memory of Jesus Christ. The church should be like its God. In what it is and does as well as in what it says, it should answer the world's questions and show the authenticity of God as love. But in so many ways the church is unlike the God revealed in Jesus Christ...
>
> Instead of enabling people to share in a communal journey contributing freely to the cause of the kingdom, it inhibits people, keeping them in a state of dependency, like a flock of sheep! (Kane: 21)

Fundamentalism

As we have seen in chapter two, in the last decades of the 19th century some Christians responded to the challenges of changes in society by asserting the need to accept Scripture and tradition without question. This was to result in the fundamentalism of the first decades of the 20th century in both Catholic and Evangelical circles. The term 'fundamentalism' was first used by the American

Protestant, Curtis Lee Laws in the Baptist journal *Watchman-Examiner* in 1920. It had developed from the search for Protestant Christian fundamentals that could be adhered to when resisting the tide of theological liberalism (especially in regard to the Bible) that, as they perceived it, threatened to engulf the faith and practice of the church. They objected to the way biblical scholars were subjecting scripture to historical and literary criticism, and the concern to relate the faith to modern culture. They also felt they should stand fast against the continuing developments in science that appeared to conflict with Scripture as literally interpreted – the Darwinian theory of evolution was especially condemned. At around the same time (1907) Pope Pius X was making his declarations in his encyclical *Lamentabili Sane* ("With Truly Lamentable Results"), to exclude various scholars whom he named "Modernists" in the Catholic Church. Pius was alarmed at the introduction of free thought in the universities. In 1925 the "Scopes Trial" in Dayton, Tennessee revealed the extent to which fundamentalists would go. Those anxious to ensure the teaching of a literalist understanding of Genesis had introduced into the state laws of Tennessee, and other southern states, a law banning the teaching of Darwinism in state schools. In defying the ban, Scopes set the scene for a national debate on the subject.[70]

Today fundamentalist Christians face yet another cultural challenge – this time in the form of a postmodern society of free choice. Protestant Fundamentalists persist in the literal interpretation of Scripture, epitomised in their attitude to Genesis 1 to 6 (the Creation to the story of Noah). Calling themselves Creationists, they maintain that the Theory of Evolution is in error, and claim scientific evidence to back this stance. But since the 1960s the postmodern world has called into question many other religious and social conventions and beliefs, especially in Europe. Fundamentalists have raised their opposition, seeing some of the reasons for this development rising out of the failure of organized religion and it's acceptance of liberal views.[71]

The Roman Catholic Church is having to cope with a right wing epitomised by the "Priestly Society of St. Pius X"[72] which grew out of opposition to Vatican II. It was inspired by Archbishop Marcel Lefebrve, and sought to preserve the Latin mass and other old traditions of the church, and seeks to apply the injunctions of Pius X to the Church now. By 1970 the Archbishop had founded his own seminary in Ecône, Switzerland. In 1974 Lefebrve made a declaration against neo-Modernists and neo-Protestant tendencies that led to the, "demolition of the Church, to the ruin of the priesthood, to the destruction of the Holy Sacrifice of the Mass and the Sacraments, the disappearance of religious life and to naturalist and Teillardian teaching in universities, seminaries and catechetics, a teaching born of Liberalism and Protestantism many times condemned by the magisterium of the Church".[73]

The impact of these Christian fundamentalisms is not as great in Europe as it is in the United States, but nevertheless, has a considerable influence on current evangelism. They are especially keen to teach their doctrine to young people, and have interests in schools and universities. In America there are whole universities founded on fundamentalist doctrine. They unashamedly aspire to the "tight knit" view of Christianity that draws a sharp distinction between church and world. The common trait of religious fundamentalism has been identified by Marty and Appleby's "Fundamentalism Project"[74] as militancy. Fundamentalists fight *back* against the challenges to their core identities. They fight *for* "the world view they have inherited or adopted and which they constantly reinforce". They fight *with* "a particularly chosen repository of resources" from the past which become their fundamentals. They fight *against* the 'outsider' who may be "the infidel, the agent of antithetical sacred powers, the modernizer", but also "the friendly messenger who seeks compromise." They fight *under* God (or some transcendent reference). (Marty 1991: ix-x)

Accordingly, the energies of the fundamentalist movements are directed three ways. First in sustaining the beliefs and practices within their own fellowships. They concentrate on ensuring they are pure and untainted by any new innovations or concessions. Secondly, they work against non-fundamentalist approaches outside their fellowship. They challenge "liberal" churches or "dialogical" theology, so they attack other Christian groups and seek to discredit those who give them support. This includes both those who teach "liberal" Christianity themselves, or the church leaders who allow them. Thirdly, they proselytize among young people in particular. In America this is frequently done with great razzmatazz: outdoor festivals, televangelism, tent missions and other events. These happen less frequently in Europe but in Britain where there are such events and outreaches they tend to attract young people who are already members of churches. The impact on the unchurched is not so great because of the natural distrust postmodern youngsters have. Nevertheless, in a frightening world where there is so much fear of being left out, or persecuted, the temptation for young people to join something that looks strong and popular can be great – especially if your friends are involved.

Fundamentalism is not, of course, restricted to Christianity. All religions have their fundamentalist off-shoots, that manifest the traits identified by the the Fundamentalism Project. They are concerned to promote purity of religion and oppose the "corrupt and licentious ways" of the postmodern world. This is currently most manifest in Islamic fundamentalism, but young people of all cultures are subject to such extremists.

Fundamentalism, however, is not the answer to introducing young people to the grace and love of God. I believe it is quite the opposite and, in fact, dangerous.

First, because it is not actually (despite its protestations) God orientated and misleads people into a false sense of security. It is not centred on God as he can be fully known, because it is so wrapped up in preserving "truth" that it is closed to the dynamic freedom of the Spirit. (Some fundamentalists may manifest signs of the Spirit but at the same time they are closely controlled. If someone were to say things under the influence of the "Spirit" that does not conform to the fundamental creed then this will be rejected, or even condemned). These churches are highly structured and hierarchical in nature and exercise careful authority. Central to these churches are their leaders. Young people who are caught up in this kind of religion are kept away from an empowering, liberating God. The people who are involved with such religion have ceased to travel on a spiritual journey to discover the wonders of God and grow into his love because they believe they have arrived at the Ultimate Truth (Jesus Christ as revealed in Scripture) already, beyond which there is nothing more to discover. To explore is to deviate, all that is left for them is to obey. Apart from being very detrimental to their spiritual health, I believe this is also dangerous because, through blind obedience, they can come under the influence of human power and abuse.

A second reason fundamentalism is dangerous is that it increases the scepticism of young people towards religion as a whole. At first glance, it may seem that fundamentalist type religion with its large rallies and prominent youth congregations has a strong appeal. But, in truth, the positive impact in Britain is nothing like that in America, and even less significant in France. European young people tend to be highly critical and to think deeply about the implications of their actions. They are aware of other cultures, languages and ethnic groups and are instinctively suspicious of the possibility of ulterior motives. For example, the troubles in Northern Ireland over the last three decades have had a deep impact. The sight of ranting clergymen encouraging the divisive sectarianism of the province has done Christianity no favours at all. I meet people today who are worried about allowing their children and young people to get involved in anything religious, even mainstream churches, because they are nervous of what it might do to them. Some feel it is better to be on the safe side and go with the New Age which is not organized or packaged, even if what is on offer does not wholly satisfy their spiritual quest. This is completely understandable if Christianity is presented in black and white, all or nothing, terms. It disturbs me greatly – no that is not strong enough! – it upsets me and makes me angry when I see young people, and not so young, frightened off by over enthusiastic, narrow minded religion. Someone on the brink of knowing God in all his love who is "got at" by those with a fundamentalist energy can be put off from exploring Christianity again for decades. "Religion", one group of Christian youngsters reported, "has a bad name". This makes it hard for them to interest others in the church. As someone who conducts funerals, I come across this phenomenon many times. I find people who have spent a life time searching for God on their own because someone, somewhere in the past, has damaged their willingness to trust any Christian. Those who are bereaved frequently express their surprise that Christianity can speak of so much love and hope! It is a pity that it takes a death for people to realize how much God can offer through the Church. My fear is that increasing numbers of people will not resort to the Church even in these times.

A third reason fundamentalism is undesirable is that it's very narrowness stifles the search for God. Some maintain that Christians need to be "definite" and preach "certainty". They warn against what they see as lukewarm Christianity. They claim that in an uncertain world people are crying out for "clear" thinking, by which they mean something that has already been thought through, prepackaged and crisp. But God does not play it that way. The world he created is not tidy and succinct, it is fuzzy at the edges and often unpredictable. He plays hide and seek with us because he wants us to seek him and find him, and keep finding him anew. This world is one that grows, evolves organically – yes according to scientific laws – but not in a totally predictable way. When each person is conceived no-one can say which of the millions of sperm cells will arrive at the egg first. No two of us are alike. The possible combinations of life that make up the world are enormous, yet within it all dwells the Spirit of God, God at every conceivable interface, creating and recreating. This is no solid, unchanging, impassible structure as the fundamentalists insist on having it. If we want people to reach out, or reach in, and touch the God who in-dwells them and participate in him, a narrow fundamentalism will not do. We need to explore a relationshipwith God. As we travel through life so we will understand more of his presence within it. We do our young people a great dis-service if we try to do too much more than open up minds to the possibilities of God for them. Chris Rogers, writing for young people, says: "Please don't get me wrong and think that I've got all the answers. I question constantly; its a journey, a walk with our Maker. All I know is that God will give us the answers we need and will carry us on the road. God loves a quizzical mind that is walking and chatting with him over a mind that thinks it knows all and never even jumps on the road." (Rogers, 7).

Enough has been said to point out some of the problems, now we need to move on to look at ways that people living in today's fluid culture will find helpful; ideas of presenting faith that will lead them to engage with the things that God offers through Christian faith, worship and living.

7. Meaningful ways of Living and Believing in a Fluid World

In seeking ways that will enable people, especially young people, rooted in a postmodern worldview to discover what Christianity brings, we have to look for approaches that both respect and grow from that worldview. As we have seen, conventional church, or fundamentalist responses do not work. At best they pick up a few along the wayside. If the future of Christianity only lies in unmovable and monolithic expressions of spirituality then it is doomed to make no real contribution to people's search for God. Christianity is a dynamic faith derived from a dynamic God that is always the same but never the same, is utterly dependable and trustworthy but is vital and active, to be found in the interfaces of life as well as gloriously transcendent. He causes people to grow, guiding them into new insights and greater understanding as they journey through life. In truth, God is more in tune with a fluid world than with a static one.

Immersed in the World

If God is "dialogic", as Atherton explains (see above in chapter four), then the first thing we need to do is involve ourselves with humanity as it is. Christians need to abandon the concept of a safe church represented by my analogy of the walled garden, and be immersed in the world. We need to recognize that God and his followers are not only "in" the world but part and parcel with it. It is a fallacy to think that Christians can be somehow detached. We are of the world, products of our genes and upbringing, our environment, education and culture. In fact, if we are to be Christ-centred then we must be part of the world. What we require is a perception that is more about the Kingdom of God, God's rule both on earth and beyond it, than an unconnected or insulated Church. The world that God created and creates is not to be confused with a "dominion of darkness" (Colossians 1:13). Many Christians do not pay enough attention to the Kingdom, although they pray for it daily when they say, "Thy Kingdom come". They have an idea that the Kingdom of God is only in the future, but Jesus says: "The Kingdom of God has come upon you" (Matthew 12:28). As C. H. Dodd explains in *The Apostolic Preaching and its Developments,* the Kingdom of God and the *eschaton* (ultimate fulfilment) are dynamic, active concepts including both present and future in what he calls "realized eschatology" (Dodd, 85).

So Christians need to be involved in the world at every level. They do not sally forth from a "walled garden", but they live and work and play with everyone else. That is why I am troubled by Christians who club together. I am disappointed, for example, by directories of Christian tradespeople whom church members are encouraged to use. We should not treat those who are not "card-carrying-Christians" as if they were outsiders and of less worth. Let us be a full part of the communities in which we live.

Nor is it true that the world is a dark, evil place, full of sinners, whilst the church is full of light and goodness. The church contains some pretty sinful people whilst some of our most caring people have no religious affiliation. (The recent scandals concerning paedophilia make us all too aware that its open fellowship attracts those wanting to gain access to vulnerable people. It is not just those on the fringe of membership either.)

So if there is caring to be done let us do that alongside others. For example, why start up our own "in house" associations for single parents or drop in youth centres if they are already established in the neighbourhood. There are two reasons, I believe, why this is a tempting proposition for some churches. The first is that it enables us to tell ourselves, and others, that we are being an active, caring church because we have a tangible, measurable commodity. (The fact that we have our own association, however, does not say anything for its quality, which is critical). The second reason is to use the association as a means of proselytism, as a way to lever single parents or young people, or whoever, into the church fellowship. Note that I do not use the term "evangelism" which is a very important part of being a Christian. Sharing the Gospel is not the same thing as setting about "building up the numbers of the fellowship" by manipulating people that come for one thing and giving them another. If we say we wish to help single parents, then that is what we should set out to do and nothing more. Of course, that does not prevent us from being willing to talk about our faith, nor does it exclude arranging something for single parents or young people to come and think and talk about the Gospel, so long as it is clearly labelled as such. The initiative should always remain with the inquirer. The point that I am seeking to make here is that Christians should be involved within the community alongside everyone else without condition or ulterior motive. They should be observed as genuinely caring and honestly concerned for the whole community, loving in the same way God loves us. (John 13.34). Trust is a difficult thing to earn and Christians should seek to be as genuinely trustworthy as the God they proclaim. Unfortunately that has not been the case among a number of people who call themselves Christian, and that has made, and continues to make, it very difficult for those who seek to care as God cares.

I am reminded of a socialist councillor in Leeds who was a member of what we would call today, "Old Labour". She was a woman with an ideal and worked very hard indeed to improve the lot of the people she represented. There was a youth club in the area that did sterling work in difficult circumstances on a rather bleak council estate. Both she and I were on the management committee; I as a representative of the local Christian churches and she as a councillor. On first meeting she told me in no uncertain terms that she had never come across a church that did any good. The churches she knew were not really interested in improving people's lives here on earth. I remember speaking of empowering people to build some faith in themselves and telling her that the church wanted to be involved in the club for the same reasons she was there. She remained sceptical. It took three years of working alongside, caring for the volunteers, weeping with the hurt, mending relationships (always under strain in such an environment), helping to secure finance, looking to expand the work into residential care for post sixteen teenage girls at risk, and generally being around with enthusiasm for the work, to change her mind. The truth is that a lot of the church is just like that, but it is also true to say that much of it isn't. It disappoints me that reports like *Faith in the City* and *Faith in the Countryside* can be so much ignored (or even criticised) by such a large proportion of the faithful. It is a tribute to the Church of England that it set up the Urban Fund, and it is vital that its future be secured because its job has by no means been completed (if it ever will). The allocation of resources is an issue to which we shall return.

Caring is not something needed just in the cities. In one rural English county, Churches Together received a request from the chief executive of what is now called Community Action. Community Action, affiliated to Action for Communities in Rural England (ACRE)[75] seeks to facilitate community caring in remote areas, being concerned with housing, transport, local facilities (like shops and post-offices) and the considerable problems of the farming community. She wanted a church representative on the executive committee because, as she rightly pointed out, the church had more widespread local contacts and groupings than any other local association. She got what she wanted. The Anglican diocese appointed a Rural Affairs Chaplain (myself) to work one day a week. The expense (a minute proportion of the Diocesan budget) was, however, a bone of contention with those who could not see the point of having someone appointed to work at county level in this field. But this was not an argument that worried the Women's Institute, CPRE[76] or Parish and District Councils who understood the benefits of awareness raising and networking. Even those who live in the countryside are not always mindful of the fragility of the farming community, even after the 2001 outbreak of Foot and Mouth Disease. If the church had not responded in the late 1980s with a central office, the Arthur Rank Centre (based at the National Agricultural Centre at Stoneleigh in Warwickshire), it would have been in a much more difficult position than it was to launch a fund[77] to help farmers made destitute by the devastation caused by the disease.

The Church has been involved in this kind of care throughout its life, and is deeply involved in it today. There are many who commit many hours and much giving of money to this work, a lot of which is done in and through existing organisations as it should be. Nearly every caring group, whether it be for people who are sick, poor, lonely, bereaved, housebound, homeless, addicted to drugs or alcohol, projects such as drop in centres, family contact centres or for any number of "social diseases", have Christians within them. Much of this work, as is the nature of it, goes unsung. Nevertheless, it does not appear as a central item of Church meetings very often. Looking down the agendas of the Church of England General Synod, for example, one could be forgiven for thinking that the issue of social care is peripheral. This goes for churches at all levels. Church organization, membership, buildings and finances appear to be the main concerns of the mainstream denominations. Sometimes the Church can come across as quite heartless. The regulations, for example, surrounding what may or may not be placed in a churchyard and the faculty procedures. At one time it was almost impossible (on the grounds of aesthetics) to get permission in some dioceses to install sound systems to help older people hear what was taking place.[78] People missed out on the benefits whilst the complicated (and presumably expensive) legal procedures were gone through. So for all that the Church is involved in the community, it still appears to put more concern into maintaining the organization and keeping historic buildings safe than into loving one's neighbour. If the Church is to be able to present the Gospel effectively in a postmodern age then it is going to have to address seriously this perception at all levels. Can this be done? If it cannot, then it will die. Some believe that this process of dying is inevitable, trusting, of course, in a resurrection in which it will be re-formed – a very Christian model. But through such a process there will inevitably be much that is good that will be lost along with the bad or inappropriate (including the social caring that is currently in progress), and a generation or two of people will miss out on the "Good News". The Church has an urgent obligation to present itself as relevant. It is not yet too late. There is still much good will that should not be squandered. But the situation is critical.

It is interesting to note that in the area of social responsibility (the French call it "*solidarité*") there is a remarkable coming together. Work of this nature is often set up and administered ecumenically. When the church members come out of their separate close fellowships to work and to love one another as God has loved them, the differences of affiliation and all the problems associated with "solid" or "static" church tend to disappear. In the process of being the church in the world, ("making or doing Church" – another French expression – *faire Église*), the Church is being re-formed, renewed to become the "salt of the earth" (Matthew 5.13). If the Church has a future it lies immersed in the world, God's world, into which, as Jesus Christ, he was born and for which he died.

Church as an Organism

One of the greatest problems for the church today is that it has become an organization demanding much administration with a detailed constitution. The Roman Catholic Church and Church of England are the prime examples, but all the mainstream churches have gone down the same route. They may have begun with being prophetic, but have become bogged in the mire of thousands of rules, regulations and conventions. It is true that all institutions need to be organized – but is the Church intended by God to be an institution or an organization? St. Paul describes the Church as the "Body of Christ" (1 Corinthians 12.12-31). A body is not an "organization" but an "organism". An organism is something that grows. It is dynamic and alive. An organization is static and, by its very nature, intended to be solidly structured. Somehow the Church must gain the courage to let go of too much ordering and become, once again, an organism. It must concentrate its efforts on doing church in the midst of the world by revising the agendas and determining its aims to be clearly along lines of ministry and mission. When I ponder on the achievements and the quality of Christian caring and outreach being done by Christian people that I know, I can truly say that the vast majority of this was never considered by any part of the organization of the Church. The old lady receiving a welcome call from a neighbour, a youth work volunteer sitting alongside a young girl caught up in an unseemly world because her single parent mother is often out drunk, those who run children's holiday clubs, lead bible studies or visit people in hospital rarely refer to the institution as such because they arise from local need and are locally inspired. Things that are infused from above must involve orders or recommendations, and at least some red tape. Most of the youth work I have known is home produced even if it takes advantage of regional or nationally organized events. These local initiatives are "organic" developments that require little "long-term" planning, address themselves to the perceived needs and use the opportunities that present themselves. They involve the minimum of paper work.

The Church at national and diocesan/district levels needs to recognize this, resource it, and think of ways it can stimulate more of this sort of activity. People at these levels should ask themselves how effective they are really being to the Body of Christ, as agents for the Kingdom, at these levels? Some of them may bravely conclude that the Church as an organism needs them to operate in a different way. The guiding principle in everything will be for every individual or group within the structures of the institution to ask themselves and God, daily, "What should I be doing to proclaim the Gospel through ministry and mission in God's world – the world in which we find ourselves?" An organic Church is always orientated towards God because the future is in his hands, not ours.

An organic Church is one which keeps before it the example of Christ and his teaching, and responds to his call to follow in total trust, "Take nothing for your journey, no staff, nor bag, nor bread, nor money – not even an extra tunic.", says Jesus (Luke 9.3), with the assurance:

> "Why are you talking about having no bread? Do you still not perceive or understand? Are your hearts hardened? Do you have eyes, and fail to see? Do you have ears, and fail to hear? And do you not remember? When I broke the five loaves for the five thousand, how many baskets full of broken pieces did you collect?" They said to him, "Twelve." "And the seven for the four thousand, how many baskets full of broken pieces did you collect?" And they said to him, "Seven." Then he said to them, "Do you not yet understand?" (Mark 8.17-21)

This postmodern age gives us opportunities and freedom to explore and experiment, to use our imagination and venture out in faith, both as individual Christians and as a body. Are we not being given a new life, a chance to shrug off the baggage of past centuries and travel light once more? Can we have a light touch as God has with us? A story which I recently published in the local church magazine about growing parsnips seems to have made an impression. It goes like this.

> Two years ago I tried growing my own parsnips. I followed the instructions on the packet of seeds to the letter. They came up alright, but in the Autumn, when it was time for harvesting, they were still no bigger than a pencil. I left a couple to see if they would benefit from another season, but they did a wonderful job of flowering while their roots remained small and became really woody. A failure! I was going to have to go back to spuds and beans. I had tried, but it was quite clear my garden was not right for them (or so I liked to think). Yet that was not the end of the story. One of the ones that had flowered had evaded being uprooted, and, very quietly, it managed to seed. When I came to see where to put the beans this year there was a lovely bed of fresh young parsnips – already, in April, the size of my pencil! By Autumn I should have some really nice specimens. All I need to do is to keep half an eye on them. Leaving things up to nature is often best – the gardener with the light touch who works with nature is usually the most successful. However, for all sorts of reasons, human beings are often bent on independence. This may come from a reluctance to share, or fear of being taken advantage of, or simply through sheer cussedness! But, if my garden is going to produce what it's capable of, I cannot rely

> on my actions alone. I cannot make a single new cell, let alone a whole plant, grow. My job as a gardener is to provide the touches that help plants prosper by allowing them room, watering and feeding. But if I overdo the weeding, watering or fertilizing – if I am too heavy-handed – my efforts will be counter-productive. Those with "green-fingers" are those who treat plants with sensitivity and patience, working with them and encouraging rather than always digging up, moving or handling them. That's the way God attends to us. He doesn't treat us like a drill sergeant, he has a light touch and allows us to blossom with the joy of discovery and achievement. We are called to relate to the world in exactly the same way. "As you have sent me into the world, so I have sent them into the world" (John 17:18), Jesus prays.

Organised Church is far too "heavy". Sadly, some people are securely enmeshed in a heavily structured, controlled, churchy environment and are isolated from the world. This is heightened by living and working in ancient buildings that connect more solidly with the past than with the present. For them, the world beyond the cloister can appear very intimidating, and it is natural for some people to want to continue to invest in secure, familiar surroundings. But if the church is to fulfil its calling to mission it cannot be confined to such places. Jesus and his disciples were out and about, always on the move, meeting people where they lived and worked – Jesus was in the world, not shut away in the Temple in a controlled and heavily regulated environment. I am not saying that we should abandon our ancient buildings and beautiful sanctums, but we must see them for what they really are. They are resources for prayer and study – and, with imagination, can be used for social outreach and evangelism too – but they must not be seen as central to what it means to be Church. As the saying goes, "home is where the heart is", and our hearts are centred in God who lives, breathes, suffers, dies and lives again in the whole of his creation.

If re-formation on these lines is hard to face at national and district levels, on the local level it is a huge challenge. No church leader can successfully keep everyone happy, and they should not aim to. Those who try it often suffer from a huge sense of failure (and worse) – as well they might because it is a task in which they cannot succeed. But our goal, the people of God, is to tell the world, in word and action, that God lives in it, loves it and, in Christ, died for it. We have to abandon all aspirations of adhering to the former structures for their own sake. Not only is it impossible to turn the clock back, it is undesirable because, for all its drawbacks, the postmodern age offers us new and exciting opportunities. I have deliberately avoided the word "shortage" in relation to the declining number of paid clergy because it assumes we wish to remain in the old forms of Church.

Could it be that God is leading us forward into a new way of doing Church? Should we be looking for something other than re-grouping our parishes into ever greater units, whatever we call them – "team ministries", "mission and ministry areas", "new parishes" – whether imposed or put together by local discussion or consultation, but always involving maps, boundaries and organization? Can we keep the imaginative ideas surrounding mission and ministry where these are based on an organic development, but forget demarkation of territory and authority? Such suggestions threaten those seeking power or control, but are a welcome release to vicars, and ministers and congregations who are burdened by ever greater organizational responsibilities.

I am reminded of the situation with the Roman Catholic Church in much of France. In recent decades the vocations to the traditional priesthood have fallen away. Some dioceses are ordaining less than one new priest every two years. This in no way compensates for the loss as older priests retire. However, there has been much rethinking in recent times forced upon the Church by the situation. Lay people have been trained to lead communities and formation has been given in basic Christian teaching. The outcome has been an unprecedented freedom for ordinary lay Christians who have gone about the task of ministry and mission with enthusiasm. The words they employ are, "sharing", "Gospel", "new life", "together", "community" and "*solidarité*" (identification with those in need). The old parishes have been dispensed with, and new arrangements (new parishes) have been put in place. Many lay Christians have grown in their new roles.

The Church in Europe is being forced to change by the strength of the postmodern culture in which it lives that has led to fewer young people willing to preserve the institution, either as clerics or laity, in its traditional forms. It is also because the Church in Europe has had its visionaries over the past fifty years both as church leaders and theologians as well as ordinary Christians. The Second Vatican Council, reports such as those I have mentioned and others besides in the Church of England, and similar moves in other mainstream churches have all made their mark. Individual contributions have come from seminal scholars from Hans Küng and Edward Schillebeeckx in the 1970s and 80s. It's amazing how popular books, both theological and practical, like John Robinson's *Honest to God* (1963) and Michael Wright's *New Ways for Christ* (1975) look so ordinary thirty or forty years on when they were quite daring in the sixties and seventies. We have come a long way, but we needed to, and we have to continue that process without succumbing to conservative and negative institutionalism insistent on preservation for its own sake.

This is addressed in two recent reports from the Church of England, *A Mission Shaped Church: Church Planting and Fresh Expressions of Church in a Changing*

Context (2004), and *A Measure for Measures in Mission and Ministry (a Review of the Dioceses).* The Churches Together in Britain and Ireland's *Presence and Prophecy: a Heart for Mission in Theological Education* has a similar approach. All these take us further down this route of greater lay involvement in a mission minded environment.

A Mission Shaped Church recognises that mission is the central activity of the church and explores ways in which the church can reach out in the present climate. It identifies fresh expressions of church and different types of church planting appropriate for the local area in which they operate. These new ways have grown up in Britain over the past 15 years or so and include manifestations of Base Ecclesiastical Communities like those of South America based on the theology of liberation: "café churches" and "cell churches", mid-week and network based churches, school based churches and youth congregations also figure. The report touches on the contentious issue of whether or not we should allow the church to be split along cultural, age or class lines. The "homogeneous unit principle" (HUP) conceived by Donald McGavran in 1955 states, "People like to become Christians without crossing racial/linguistic/class and cultural barriers". Is this a good thing? If all of us are "one in Christ" (Galatians 2:28), should not the church be so all embracing that it gathers all people in its locality under one roof, irrespective of cultural or other differences? I have held onto the principle of drawing all together in one family for over twenty years of ministry, but I have to admit failure. People need to grow, they need to be challenged in worship and have as much involvement as possible. It is not easy, for instance, to do that for educated, middle class people with an ear for classical music on the one hand, and young people from working class backgrounds into pop music and computer games on the other. Add to the mix young parents with restless toddlers and the very old with hearing difficulties hoping to gather something to prepare for the next world, and the task becomes a real challenge. I have concluded that the gains from gathering all people in one place for more than the occasional gala are out-weighed by the value of addressing individual needs. We have to meet at different times, and different lengths of times, employ different language and gear worship along different patterns. *A Mission Shaped Church* concludes:

> Thus some aspects of theology point to a culture-specific social expression of the gospel. Other aspects challenge us to build bridges of unity and reconciliation between such groups. The answer may be to accept initial cultural similarity while seeking gradual cultural diversity, expressed in interdependence between groups unlike one another. (pg. 109)

A Mission Shaped Church makes recommendations for diocesan and ecumenical planning. It speaks of leadership and training which should be for both lay and clerical ministry recognizing individual gifts but emphasize cross-cultural evangelistic thinking.

A Measure for Measures adopts this principle of mission in addressing church policies and legislation in respect of buildings and clergy deployment. The report recognizes that "the current situation is one calling for 'pioneering' mission as well as 'pastoral' mission" (pg. 3). The thrust of the report, in dealing with the institution's functions, is to simplify and free the church from red tape and structures that stifle its missionary character.

A highlight is its theological appendix by the Revd. Dr. Malcolm Brown. Brown recognizes the cultural challenges of our times, but he is concerned not to go too much down the line of accepting a culture of consumer choice as adequate for Christian expression. The supermarket should not become, "the paradigm of all human decision making", he warns. In this he is right, for, as we have seen, young people as well as older ones, are looking to the church to proclaim truth and faith and not to shy away from demands of discipleship. Brown writes: "... the good life, in the love of God, is not about getting what you want but doing what faith, conscience and love compel." "Nevertheless", he continues, "the imperatives of mission mean that the church is obliged to take account of the consumer mentality in its encounter with contemporary culture. If the gospel is to be heard, it must connect in some way with the categories and vocabulary of people as they are, and yet it must also call them to a more abundant life and to richer, truer, stories about being human under God." (pg. 117). Our object in taking urgent notice of the cultural assumptions of young people in the way we address them is not to reduce the gospel to fit postmodern ideas any more than it was right that Christianity has been reduced in the past to fit into the cultures of the old English establishment.

Brown warns us about trying to make models of mission fit all contexts – suburban values, for example, should not be allowed to predominate while urban priority areas and rural villages are ignored. (pg 118). He draws our attention to the tensions between the local and the centre. "There is an important 'settlement'" in Anglicanism between the centre and the local church that places, "the contemporary carefully into the context of the historical" (pg 115). Brown's call is for the church to make visible "inward spiritual reality" that is obscured by outmoded "outward manifestations of church life" (pg 128). "The Christian task is to live authentically in the light of the knowledge of God and its grasp of the scripture and tradition ..." (pg 111). *A Measure for Measures* attempts to clear away some of the organizational complexities that have accumulated over four hundred years and more which are holding us back in our primary task to share the gospel with everyone no matter where and how they live.

The Chain of Memory

Despite all these moves in the mainstream churches in the last forty years, when I, as a parish priest, say things like those above in a local context, I am frequently accused by those already part of the church of wishing to dispense with all that has gone before. That is not the case. I am not for revolution but I do want the church to be living and active (*cf* Heb. 4:12). I have no quarrel with those who wish to preserve the good things in our history. Indeed as a European who has lived outside of Europe for some time I value our heritage and see the disadvantages of those societies which are not as rich in them as we are. I am all for keeping our old church buildings and keeping them looking beautiful. I belong to the National Trust, visit ancient castles, ruins, museums and art galleries. I am frequently found delving into classical literature or history books just as much as I am fascinated by cosmology and new scientific discoveries. This is a popular thing to do in a fluid age and not just among people like myself who can go back a bit. Young people want to know about their heritage. They enjoy talking to old people who have tales to tell of former times and wish to explore ideas and stories that can help them form their values for today. The humanities are popular among GCSE and A level students, including religious studies. What the Christian tradition brings is of the highest quality, and it is important that it is handed on to each generation. There is a "chain of memory" of which Danièle Hervieu-Léger speaks which was once about faithfulness to the institution. Hervieu-Léger describes a change in which modern individualism has completely transformed the expectations and attitudes of the contemporary "mobile believer"[79] (Hervieu-Léger 1999: 25). Contemporary believers follow new patterns of affiliation which Hervieu-Léger identifies as the 'pilgrim' and the 'convert'.[80] The 'pilgrim' can be seen in action especially among the young at Taizé, for example, or the Roman Catholic "World Youth Days" (where millions of young people converge to meet the Pope). "It reflects", says Hervieu-Léger, "in metaphorical fashion the fluidity of the individual spiritual journey" and, "corresponds to a form of religious sociability ... which orders itself under the sign of mobility and of temporary association" (Hervieu-Léger, 1999: 98). She explains:

> In fact we can speak of individualization of the religious in seeing the difference between a ritual religion which merely requires of the faithful the minute observation of the prescribed practices, and an internal religion which involves, in a mystical and ethical mode, the personal appropriation of religious truths by each believer. (Hervieu-Léger 1999:157-158)

Most believers today no longer validate their beliefs by reference to a 'validation by the institution', which is the traditional expectation of the Roman Catholic Church – a model in which each believer accepts without question the authority and teaching of religious leaders. Hervieu-Léger identifies three alternative validations of belief – 'autovalidation' ("in which the subject recognizes only him or herself as having the capacity to test the truth of what he or she believes" (Hervieu-Léger 1999: 180)), 'mutual validation' (based on personal witness and the exchange of individual experiences), and 'communitary (*communitaire)* validation' (observed in militant movements and close knit religious groups where, "the cohesion of the community witnesses for each individual the truth of the common belief"(Hervieu-Léger 1999: 183)). These validations of belief spring from the need to re-establish a new referent where the "chain of memory" has been ruptured due to the fragmentation of society in the modern (and now postmodern) age. In her work *Religion as a Chain of Memory* (1993) Hervieu-Léger asserts that these new validations almost totally eclipse, in Western Europe, the traditional institutional validations of the past. The process began with the *Lumières* of the Enlightenment and has been a growing feature of the rational modern world and the hallmark of the postmodern.

So this is no longer about the maintenance of institutional memory concerning, for example, what colour of vestment a priest should wear on the third Sunday of Advent, or whether the prayers precede the sermon or the other way round. This is about individuals, and those with whom they lead their lives, persisting in faith in the presence of God which colours all of their behaviour and beliefs. Despite the falling numbers of those attending church buildings, the Christian faith, itself, will not die out. There is so much that has been written, including the life-breathing Scriptures themselves. The phenomenon of Christianity will remain on school curricula, just as the works of the philosophers of religion and ethics are being so well received by A level students today. But if we rely only on these kinds of way of handing on the Gospel we shall lack the personal and corporate witness of what we know within ourselves – the active and real love of God that is experienced primarily in the gathered Christian community. We can testify to the power of the Spirit to bestow upon us his fruits of love, joy, peace, patience, goodness, humility, faithfulness, kindness, generosity and self-control (Galatians 5:22-23). We can talk about prayer, and actually pray with people who want to discover him. It is this that will be lost if we do not seek to change and take every opportunity to preserve the memory of the people of God in this present age. We are in grave danger of losing it because we have not yet fully woken up to the way we need to use the resources we have and to abandon the doomed fortresses of the old immutable structures. It is not too late, but the time is not far off and we must begin to set active believing Christians free to pass on the "memory" of what it is to live in and through Christ.

Where then should we put our resources of precious time and memory? We shall come to this question in a moment, but first we need to take a look at the idea of "liquid church" advanced by Pete Ward as a solution to this problem and what the New Testament church called *Koinonia.*

Church as Communion

Ward sees the future of Christianity in the western world in Church based on "communication" rather than "gathering". He refers to the way young people have taken to modern technology to keep in touch with one-another often at some distance. Mobile phones that offer cheap text messaging, together with emailing take up a considerable chunk of young people's time. "Community has not died", says Ward, "but it has changed. People still want to be with each other, they still want to feel they have significant relationships, and they still want to make a difference in other people's lives. In liquid modernity this desire is expressed through constant communication." (Ward, 88). Ward advances a network model of church: "The networked church would connect individuals, groups, and organizations in series of flows. Connection would gather round hubs and would be made of connecting nodes." (Ward, 87). This is the very way the Internet works, the epitome of modern communication that has become an essential element of liquid modernity. These "hubs" and "nodes" could be any kind of Christian activity or interest ranging from sports centres to bible study groups, music to the "ethics of business". The only limit to these is the limit to the imagination. What they would not be is solid, safe, heavy church. "The hope would be", continues Ward, "that intimacy of Christian fellowship would restore a qualitative character to the life of the church, offering genuine connection and relationship rather than what so often feels like a pretence of community." (Ward, 90). He envisages worship to be a series of varied offerings rather than the regular weekly diet of solid church. People could come along to these as they please without a congregational commitment. He refers us to the labyrinth idea in St. Paul's Cathedral, London in which people walked round to different prayer stations each offering a different focus of attention. (This idea, or variations of it, has been taken up in many places). One adaptation of this idea, suggests Ward, "is as part of a café that could use the labyrinth to offer a place for spiritual exploration and experience as well as pastries and cappuccinos." (Ward, 97). He reminds us of the informal way some Greek Orthodox congregations come and go and walk around during the service, lighting candles and kissing icons. Worship may be city wide or local but "de-centred", "worship that does not rely upon a congregational dynamic." (Ward, 94). Central to this idea of liquid church is that it has to remain constantly innovative: "Liquid church would see that the short term and an offer for a limited period only is an essential part of making it special. This is particularly the case when we are dealing with the press. The culture of media-based publicity relies upon what is new. The regular habits of solid church don't cause any great stir in the press." (Ward, 93)

I believe Ward has done Christians a great deal of service with his vision, his "dream" as he calls it, of a Church committed to living in liquid modernity. I believe we would do well to put into practice ways of doing church that use a network of centres of interest. We should use every bit of our imagination in this regard and we should be prepared, at both national and local levels, to resource the ideas of inspired people. Much of what Ward suggests, as he acknowledges, is already happening – albeit mostly as side activities. There are many people with ideas, but they often find themselves under-resourced, ignored or even discouraged by people fearful of change. If Ward has gone any way to inspire church leaders to see the virtue of such new ways of doing church then we need to be very grateful to him.

However, I do have reservations with the idea of liquidity in the way that Ward envisages it. I do not see why it is not possible to have, in a postmodern society, all the ideas that Ward speaks of in terms of communication and innovative worship and hubs of common interest alongside the local congregation. Indeed, in a world of choice, should not the offer of 1662 evensong, for example, be on the spiritual shelf so long as there are sufficient people wishing to buy it? Those who participate in such a choice, however, should be aware that their preferences could not and should not be the "norm". There will always, however, be a consideration of time and resources and those with specialist interests (such as 1662 evensong) need to be willing to look to the interests of others before their own (Philippians 2.4). The guiding principle, as always, is the mission and ministry of the Church.

But the retention of the local church with its congregation is important for more reasons than respecting choices of older generations. It centres around the concept of the "communion", of a sense of belonging to something that is more than a current interest or one-off gathering. Community may be expressed through the use of modern technology, or massive festivals but it is also expressed in belonging to something that has solid substance, a substance that is organic. The members of the early New Testament Church "devoted themselves to fellowship" (Acts 2.42). The Greek word for fellowship used is "*koinonia*" which R. P. C. Hanson (following L. S. Thornton[81]) explains, "is the focus of a new relationship between God and man in Christ. It includes sharing goods in common, collecting funds to support the poverty-stricken Christians in Jerusalem (in the course of which James, Cephas and John give the right hand of fellowship to Paul) and, later, the breaking down of the barrier between Jew and Gentile ..." (Hanson: 70). It seems to me that such *koinonia*, fellowship or communion, is central to what it means to be Christian. *Communion* cannot be replaced by *communication* no matter how advanced and accessible.

I recall a story that was told me about a little girl who woke up frightened in the middle of the night. Her parents came and cuddled her and settled her down to sleep again but she was reluctant for them to leave. Her mother found a nice soft teddy bear that she had got for Christmas. “He was given to you by Daddy who loves you very much”, said her mother. “Yes”, replied the little girl aware that her father was asleep in the next room, “but teddies don’t have skin on”. It may be good to get the news from our friends and family on email. Our young people communicate much more than they did because it is so much easier. We know what they are doing (or what they are willing to tell us!) what their concerns are and their joys. We can do this instantly because they carry their phones around with them, so whether they are in Winchester or Brighton, Manchester or Durham, France or America we can say “Hi”. We can even exchange pictures at the press of a button. In fact we can communicate the same message to dozens of our friends at the same time (hundreds if we have them). Now this last bit is indicative of something very important. It shows that this is about “communication” rather than “communion”. The little girl’s Daddy might indeed love her very much, but however close the teddy bear is it is only a symbol of that love. It conveys that love, but in a detached sort of way. The girl knows instinctively the difference between symbolism and reality.

This is also revealed in the way we feel when something happens to someone we love (they are taken ill or have had some bad news) we want to be with them. There was a story on BBC 2 of a Welsh family that moved to Melbourne, Australia. There they had a dream house, a wonderful life compared to the opportunities available to them in Wales, but what they missed more than anything else was family. When grandfather was taken ill they were greatly distressed. There was nothing they could actually do for him in a practical sense, he had plenty of other people to look after him. They could speak on the telephone and exchange pictures and even presents through the post which takes only a few days. Through the Internet it is possible to arrange flowers to be sent within the hour. But none of this is any replacement for actually being there. We need “communion” as well as “communication”.

Of course, we can have a transitory communion with those we encounter within the fluid world. It could be argued that if our interest was cycling, we could come together as a Christian cycling group and make a cycling pilgrimage and that, in a meaningful way would be communion within a model of liquid church. We might, as two or three meeting together in Christ’s name, actually celebrate communion in bread wine together. This would be an authentic expression of church. All this is true, but the provisional nature of the ever changing community does not allow us to grow effectively in our communion. If the Church is to be always innovative then relationships may never reach real depth. In the cycling club analogy, it might be that two of the young people with a passion for bikes strike up a passion for each other. They could decide that this was something just for the duration of the trip, or they could express an interest in continuing that relationship and allowing it to deepen and mature. This may not prove easy since the interest that brought them together may have drawn them from different parts of the country, even different countries. If they are serious, one of them, at least, will have to move, and as the relationship continues it will take precedence over the common interests they share. Eventually a family may result which stays together, not just because they want to do the same things, but because they simply belong to one another. Our society may be a fluid one, but within the liquid there are solid particles that cling together. The Church needs to recognise this fact, and be aware that for many people local churches not only promote family commitment, but become families themselves. Within the Church family people belong to God and also to each other.

It is here that the sacraments of Baptism and Holy Communion take on their full significance. Through them God welcomes and nurtures the body of the Church as family, as communion. If the people who seek God are to grow effectively in Christ they need to be rooted in communion surrounded by others also growing. This does not mean, of course, that individuals in a liquid world will spend all of their lives in one place and attending one church. They will move around and meet others and learn from them in a new environment. The family is both extended and local. But when people move they will come across living and loving communion in the form of congregations whose members already know each other. New people can be included in a preexisting fellowship and feel "at home". The danger here, as always, is that we may become inattentive and too comfortable and slip back into a cosy fellowship that is hard for people to break into. The church fellowship, as a bishop preached at an induction of a new priest, exists "to comfort the disturbed and disturb the comfortable". Mission should be at the heart of every individual Christian and congregation. But a congregation which recognizes that it is a local expression of the wider Church, the Body of Christ, will be inclusive, and offer the communion which is at the heart of the Gospel, reflected within the Trinity and demonstrated in the Incarnation. Pete Ward's concept of "liquid church", dispensing with solid congregations, does not allow this, and it is difficult to see how in the Church that he proposes, there can be any real chain of Christian memory. He suggests resource centres and exhibitions, but again they lack the "family" contact with meaningful communion.

A liquid church that is not rooted in such communion is open to another liquid expression, "watered down". Ward develops his theory from a properly anchored understanding of what it means to be Christian, but my concern is whether those that live Christianity solely through his liquid church will inherit the theological discipline and Christian commitment that he has. One of the dangers is that we shall head back into a super fluid religious existence epitomized by Don Cupitt's "Sea of Faith".[82] Here we can say nothing of God, communion, or the meaning of human existence. Although Christianity was Cupitt's starting point, the "Sea of Faith" ideas are no longer Christian or even theist. The Sea of Faith Network website declares that "God is not an objective reality" and "all religious faith is a human creation", no different from music, poetry or painting. We are left to "make our own meaning, create our own purpose and find ways of working out our own salvation".[83] But a postmodern culture is crying out for meaningful narratives, and the Christian narrative should be, and can be, handed down the generations in all its richness through a community of faith. Let people in the present age choose, explore and buy, and let us ensure they have something solid, which includes a communion in which they can experience God as well as read of him – a communion in which we are no longer vulnerable to the whims of the market and fashion or susceptible to exploitation.

Positioning People and Resources to Connect with Young People

One of the biggest concerns in the chain of memory, therefore, is the Church's mission to the young, and its solidarity with the world and its needs. If we fail to connect with society in these areas then the chain of Christian memory will be broken. Surely then this should be of paramount importance in the way we use our assets. As I have already indicated, virtually all of the churches' financial resources are directed at maintaining the organized church, and that is also true of the talents and time of Christian individuals.

One of the things we discovered on our sabbatical tour in the Spring of 2004 was that there were very few paid youth workers among the churches. Those that exist are either at area level and are shared across hundreds of local churches or are financed wholly by the local churches. This last option is only possible for the most well off of church communities, even if it is financed by a group of churches coming together. To make a real impact a Christian youth worker should not be asked to work too widely. Wherever a person is truly committed to working with young people, no matter whether or not they be relatively young themselves, there will always be young people who respond. If young people do not feel connected with the church in anyway then it is often because the church has not provided someone whose sole job it is to be there for them. To ask local church clergy to take on this role while they are trying to lead or minister to the whole congregation and community (or more likely congregations and communities) is like asking a driver to read stories to the children in the back seat of a car. He or she can only do it if he or she keeps one hand on the wheel, one on the book, one eye on the road and the other on the children and yells at the top of his or her voice. This is difficult and dangerous and liable to failure. Rectors, vicars, ministers and priests "in charge" are regularly put into this position. As they decrease in number, so they find themselves charged with the oversight of more and more churches and people in ever wider areas. Since the numbers of young people offering themselves to serve in such positions is declining the model of church with the omni-competent, all-encompassing "parson" cannot be long sustained. Of course, it is recognised in the models of "shared", or "mutual" ministry that clergy should not always be in the driving seat, but parish priests and ministers are trained to be there to advise and pray with those who are, and to enable the sacramental sharing that is central to communion. Even in the most enlightened parish, a priest cannot pay special attention to only one or two areas of ministry. In practice, therefore, incumbent clergy for the most part have little hands on with mission and ministry with the young outside the congregations. But if young people are to hear the Gospel then the work among them cannot be done as a sideline to other business. This work is the most pressing of all and the resources should follow it. If parish clergy can be removed from the "driving seat" – a position which can be replaced by the communion itself – could some not be appointed specifically to work in youth outreach?

In fact, finding Christian men and women in their twenties willing to work with young people is not as difficult as finding new people to take on the role of parish ministers. If for every vicar that cannot be replaced we were to employ a youth worker in his/her stead, the impact would be enormous. Youth ministry could also become a specialism within the role of an ordained minister, and it would help young people to see themselves as priests or deacons. I believe the problem of recruitment for the ordained ministry has as much to do with the way we use our ordained ministers by giving them open-ended responsibilities (general practitioner expectations) as it is to do with ordination itself.

If the Church is really committed to handing on the memory of the Christian gospel to young people it must take the challenge of the allocation of resources seriously. Indeed we have no other choice. Every diocese, district and local church should make it a priority to seek to train and employ youth officers in at least every main centre throughout their area. They could, and should, do this on an ecumenical basis, and they should do it with the vision of the Kingdom of God before them rather than an idea of building up church numbers in any particular building or organization. I have no doubt that young people will eventually come together to worship, but they will probably do it in larger groups and take little notice of denominational divisions.

The common response to such a proposition from many church leaders at the decision making ends of organized church is to declare any idea that needs major reallocation of resources unworkable. The fact is, they will say, that so much of the finances of the church are already committed and cannot be readily transferred. My response to that is that unless the work among young people becomes a major commitment *now*, then in a few years' time there will be no more income to haggle about. Those older people who feel that they should be allowed to put their money into maintaining a church that is not engaging with the young are doing them a massive disservice. If they know the wonderful love, hope and goodness of God, how dare they not be prepared to do all they can to pass on that Good News to those who need to have it made available for them, even at the risk of their own discomfort.

On the question of resources *A Mission Shaped Church* concludes: "There is an urgent need to release resources to sustain mission initiatives to the non-churched. The resources of the Church of England are understandably but disproportionately invested in inherited and traditional styles of church, which alone are no longer adequate for mission to the whole nation. Strategies are needed to establish new resources and transfer some existing resources for new initiatives." (pg. 148).

I have been privileged to meet a number of Christians deeply involved in working with young people who manage to live on a shoe string to enable them to make their work a priority in their lives. One Christian couple have sold their house to raise funds for the work. Another ordained as a Non-Stipendiary Minister (NSM) in the Church of England finances his ministry by taking funerals and keeping the fees. The diocese knows he does this, and in theory he shouldn't (all fees belong to the incumbent of the parish who declares them to the diocese so that they can go into the central pot), but the diocese allow this "unofficially". This is verging on the scandalous. Should there not be proper resources for this work? How can the church in the area acknowledge and affirm the work that is being done while they allow those who are most committed at local level to impoverish themselves to do it? In fact there are not enough people who are free to give in this way, people with children for example, or with other dependent relatives. The work of ministering to the young through financing full-time Christian youth workers, chaplaincies to state schools as well as fee paying ones, enhancing those based in our universities, subsidizing pilgrimages (to Taizé or Iona for example), sending youngsters on youth camps and weekends away, providing accessible resource and ideas centres, setting up local facilities such as drop in centres and the like will be a major part of the budget of a successful 21st century Church – one that is committed to sharing the Christian treasures it has to offer. One word of warning, however, to business people who demand visible returns from their investment. In a fluid society where young people move around investment in local young people may not manifest itself locally. Nor is it likely, for all the reasons mentioned above, to make much impact on the numbers of young people appearing on a Sunday morning. I will address the question of "measuring success" in the final chapter.

Formation

The word "formation" is becoming used more frequently in English in the Roman Catholic Church and others. It means more than just training, although it includes that. Formation is something that the Catholic Church in France is making a huge priority as it faces the situation in which many congregations will not see a priest for weeks at a time. The lay people are receiving formation in everything from Christian theology and Church History, to how to conduct funerals and care for each other in times of need. It includes aspects of solidarity and youth work, and other aspects of ministry such as baptism and marriage preparation. Education is a vital element in being effective communicators of the Gospel in word and action. Not only does it inform but it empowers lay Christians, both in their voluntary work and that for which the church provides finance. Those who have received training in the past – clergy, elders, Readers (who preach), teachers, pastoral assistants etc. – can and should be refreshed and updated, but opportunities should be available for all Christian people. In some dioceses and districts this is already under way with not a little interest. The Bishop's Certificate in the Diocese of Salisbury,[84] for example, or "Living Belief"[85] at Exeter University and "Theology Quest and Questions"[86] run through Sarum College. All these initiatives throughout the Church should be both encouraged and enhanced. One of the problems again is financing. Some lay Christians are having to find a substantial fee for these courses and not all of them can afford it. Dioceses recommend that parishes take the burden off individuals and help pay for this. However, this should not be done without regard for the uneven distribution of resources between one parish and another. The important element here is that the Church at all levels makes formation of its members a priority, as a means of both enriching the growth of those who already have a relationship with Christ, and enabling them to hand it on with confidence and joy.

Older People in a Fluid Environment

I have put a great deal of emphasis in this chapter on the importance of paying attention to the needs of young people. It is they who will form the next link in the chain of Christian memory. However, we cannot finish without some mention of those who are living towards the end of their lives. In the search for God these souls are just as important as younger ones. The liquid world has advantages for them too but, as we have seen, some great challenges. It is they who have to take the responsibility of handing on the memory. It can be hard for those who hanker after happy times of former days. Nevertheless, many senior citizens are discovering new freedoms and an access to the truth and joy of Christ in a way they never thought possible before. Perhaps not surprisingly, the strict and structured world they had when they were young did not suit everyone. It may have been that the church for them has been, in the past, a closed door. Living in one place all their lives, they may have been put off the church because of past history or connections. It is revealing how many older people feel freer to identify with the church after their parents have moved on. One person in her sixties admitted to me that she could never confess her faith to her mother because that would take away her hard fought independence. (He mother had "sent" her to church three times a Sunday until she was married). Her staying outside the worshipping community was part of her claim to be an individual free of her mother's constant bidding.

The postmodern era has afforded older people new opportunities to grow and achieve. One wonderful old lady I had the privilege of knowing learned to swim and received her certificate one week before her 90th birthday. This was an achievement that gave her great pleasure because it was something she never had the chance to do as a child. Her family and friends were all very proud of her – she gave them a lot of happiness. Her positive attitude and sense of adventure, together with her graciousness and joy, resulted in her receiving no less than five birthday cakes and more cards and flowers than she had room for in her one bedroomed almshouse flat. This lady wrote for the local church news and talked to many young people, passing on all the while the joy of faith. But it was not the younger generations that benefited the most, it was those of her own generation she met several times a week in the day centre, and those who called on her for a cup of tea.

Old people are, on the whole, much easier to find than younger ones. They are more often at home and it is more natural for them to receive visitors. They can, for the same reasons, be easier to forget, and the church community must be aware of keeping a weather eye open for those in this situation. Sadly not all old people are a blessing to those who meet them. Those, for instance, who believe that complaining and demanding are necessary for gaining attention are usually quite lonely. But it is never too late to discover that giving things prompts others to reciprocate spontaneously with genuine feeling. For seven years a parish priest put up with the demands and complaints of an elderly woman. She hadn't been included as much as others in things, she claimed. The person living two doors away had been called upon more than she had; that lady even had presents of cooking or flowers. This she did not believe was fair. A week before he was due to retire the priest lost his patience. Perhaps it was because he was going that gave him the courage. " I told the old so and so," he reported, " that if instead of complaining about what she hadn't received she paid some attention to giving herself, she would have a lot more friends. If her neighbour received a plate of mince pies what she needed to do was make a plate herself – and give it away. Rather than buy herself flowers she should find someone else to give some to." The woman was furious, how dare he presume to lecture her on giving! Other people were far better off than she. But after he had left she swallowed her pride and followed his advice. Of course she is still not as popular as her neighbour who has had a life time of giving, but she has begun to feel better about herself. In fact she surprised herself just how much pleasure she got from a genuine friendly smile as she presented someone with a few buns. She now shouts at people for reciprocating. "I doesn't give to get back you know!", she declares, maintaining her pride. But at heart she's a woman being re-born! It is tempting to forget the old "so and sos" in a world of choice, yet we must not. Our aim is not to collude with their selfish insularity but to enable people of all generations to understand what it means to love as God has loved us.

The story above involved a parish priest. That priest has not been replaced and the local church has had to come to terms with caring for isolated old people without leaving it up to the clergy. Of course, this process had already begun long before the priest left, first because he could not hope to look after the increasing numbers of elderly people on his own, second because he knew he had to prepare the local people of God for the future, and thirdly because he shared a vision of the church which has been variously called, "shared", "collaborative" or "mutual" ministry. In the next chapter we shall look at ways in which the local Christian community could be transformed to become the people of God in word and action in a postmodern environment.

8. Practical Steps at the Local Level

In the past, church people have tended to arrange themselves in hierarchies with the most important people at the top of the tree. For Catholics this meant that the Pope was the most eminent person of all in the ecclesiastical world. Titles were given along these lines in descending order, "His Holiness", "His Eminence", "Most Reverend", "Right Reverend", "Very Reverend", "Venerable" etc. It paralleled the secular world with, in Europe, its kings at the top, dukes and barons next followed by lesser aristocracy until one got down to the local squires. Beneath them were the freemen who owned their own patch of land, then tenant farmers, servants of various orders and, last of all, the slaves who belonged totally – body, mind and (if it could be managed) spirit to their owners. Women and children of the various orders were subservient to their men folk. Everyone knew their place. Even revolutions failed to over-turn this order. The French Revolution, in which the term "left wing" has its origins, gave rise to Napoleon. This model survived well into the 20th century, but declined as the century progressed. Today, the forms of it persist (the titles for example) but the atmosphere is very different. Fifty years ago if an Archbishop were to come to tea the whole household may well have been thrown into what my grandmother called a "tizz". The children would have been warned to be on their best behaviour and the whole family honoured because someone "high up" was deigning to dine with them. Today it is very much more likely that the person would be welcomed in much the same way as any other guest. Formality will have given way to allowing the children to "be themselves". The way the person behaves, the presence of his character, is what is going to set the family in awe rather than his title. In today's climate, heroes, pin-ups, film stars and sports personalities rise and fall according to fashion and performance.

Some believed that privilege was a God given system, especially those who were born into it, but the teachings of Jesus do not give support to this story. St. Mark records, "Then they came to Capernaum; and when he was in the house he asked them, "What were you arguing about on the way?" But they were silent, for on the way they had argued with one another who was the greatest. He sat down, called the twelve, and said to them, "Whoever wants to be first must be last of all and servant of all." (Mark 9.33-35). There are many similar passages on this theme, culminating in the example of Jesus' washing the disciples feet at the Last Supper. (John 13.2-17)

In unprecedented ways the postmodern era has dispensed with privilege and conforms much more to the ideals of the Gospel. Those who lead, serve. In the 1950s and 60s the police, teachers, doctors and priests were still put on local pedestals to be looked up to because of what they were. Nowadays these people have to earn their respect by doing a good job and being a caring servant to the community. A new culture has emerged that uses words such as "social environment", "process", "interdisciplinary", "networking", "common responsibility" and the like. This has grown both as a product of, and a response to, a fluid society. As a monolithic authoritative institution, the Church has lagged behind the rest of society, but has not of course remained unchanged. In this chapter I want to explore some of these manifestations of change and the ways they are helping with the task of passing on the Good News in a postmodern environment, and to look at ways in which this process can be enhanced. In the final chapter we shall address the question of "indicators of success", which as we have seen, have been one of the reasons for the lack of movement in the parishes.

The Ministry and Mission of the Whole People of God

In the early 1980s I was involved in an experiment in the Diocese of Ripon and Leeds to introduce "shared ministry". The idea was that ministry should not belong exclusively to the "minister" or vicar, as it had done for centuries, but be shared by lay people. Lay Ministry Teams were appointed to oversee that ministry. Tensions and misunderstandings arose between members of the Teams and elected Parochial Church Councils (PCCs), as well as between clergy and the Teams. They interfered with the old recognised order of things. A large amount of the problem was to do with the idea that the lay members of the Teams were making themselves more important than the rest because as they shared the ministry of the Vicar, so they shared in his status. The term "little vicars" was banded about. Of course the concept of a ministry that belongs to the whole congregation was theologically sound, being based on ministry in the New Testament of service. But the time had not come in many places where this was properly understood, and the introduction of "shared ministry" was surrounded by a lot of important formation and training. This began with the clergy (some of whom felt the process left them without a recognised role) and the ministry teams and PCCs. Gradually the theology has been grasped, especially by new generations who live in a postmodern society. People who do not attend church or formation sessions but nevertheless look to the church for ministry (for baptisms, marriages and funerals for example) have been more and more accepting of lay representatives. In some places it has become the norm, especially for example with preparation for marriage or baptisms of babies. Young people do not necessarily expect to see a stipendiary clergy person.

One of the developments in some dioceses of the Church of England is the ordination of Ordained Local Ministers. These are people from the area who train locally (together with a parish learning group which may well form the nucleus of a local ministry team) and remain local to the same area. They are ministers of the sacrament, that is they help the people of God to engage in the communion which binds them both to God and each other. They are not, and should never be seen to be, replacements for the old Vicar. They do not operate outside the context of the ministry of the whole church but enable that ministry as God blesses the whole communion through the sacrament. Ordained Local Ministers are not ordained to take the responsibility of witness and ministry away from the lay members of the church to which they belong, but rather to further enable it. In practice this change is always more easily understood by younger generations than older ones where tensions may still arise, but those of the intensity of the early 1980s during our first experiments are a thing of the past.

There are enormous benefits in allowing local people to accept their true responsibility. First, locals understand what works and what doesn't. They are not only conscious of the cultures which pertain and the tensions in the neighbourhood, say between one community and another, they also know individual people and their foibles. They avoid the pitfalls open to those who come in from outside.

Secondly, local people are often more effective because those from outside, as we have seen, do not come with ready made status as in former years. People often treat new ministers with suspicion before respect, especially if they think he or she represents something of the old authoritarian order. These days in some parishes, depending on their history and circumstances, it may take up to five years for sufficient trust to be built up for full acceptance. (Some of course, – those who do not display proper respect for the community – are never seen as worthy of trust). Trust, it is to be noted, is not accorded to people because they are talented but because they are seen to be honest. People instinctively respond to "WYSIWYG" and demand it. We have to be sure, not only of the truth of what is being proclaimed, but the genuineness of the people that proclaim it. The local people that they know have an immense advantage here because they are already accepted. Often they go back a long way, even from birth sometimes, and their parents and children, wives and husbands (if they have them) are also known. The impact of this cannot be underestimated – and yet for centuries their contributions in handing on the chain of Christian memory has never been formally recognized. This is changing, and must continue to change, as local people receive the opportunities to delve more and more into the power of their relationship with God and the meaning of communion.

Thirdly, local Christians use the same language as the people around them. When I lived and worked on a council estate in Leeds, I quickly learned that what I thought was standard English was often misunderstood. People from outside, in my case someone from the Midlands trained in London, needed local interpreters to understand and be understood. I recall in my first week in Leeds a young mother inquiring about (what she called "asking after") a christening for her child. I asked her for the baby's name. Her reply sounded like "Justine". I reflected on this rather unexpected name, but continued, "Does she have a middle name?". The mother took on a belligerent expression. "It's a he! And I told you, he's 'just Dean' and there in't a middle name." The churchwarden who was with me had no difficulties about this and couldn't help bursting out with laughter after seeing what I had written. Nobody in that area would dream of a name like Justine! He could see I was going to have trouble. Sometimes the problem is not just with things that are misheard, but misunderstood. The French call French words that are also used in English but mean something different "faux amis" (false friends). This is also true of nuances in English that vary from place to place. It is easy for a Vicar from outside to think he is conveying one thing but is being heard as meaning something different, and sometimes confusing people rather than clarifying the situation. More than once in a meeting I have been stopped from speaking by someone saying, "What he means is ... ". Local people do not have this problem. Of course language is only part of it, culture is just as important. Local people know which door to use ("front" or "back"), when to call to avoid meal times, and what and how to accept or decline in terms of drink or food – and a plethora of other unwritten conventions.

Fourthly, with a church full of people all engaged in ministry, it is also possible to match people more easily. For example, a young mother is likely to have much more in common with another woman than a single man who happens to be the local stipendiary minister. It is not always as simple as this, of course, but there are many occasions when ministry is more effective because it is communicated by someone with a common background, age, or problem. This is especially important in a postmodern era when the generation gap is so wide.

Above all these pragmatic reasons for lay involvement in ministry, however, is its theological *raison d'etre.* The Church is the Body of Christ and should be perceived by the community as such. The common communion should be perceived by everyone so that they can both see that God lives in his people and be attracted to it. An individual, such as a parish incumbent, no matter how wonderful she or he is, cannot do this. Ordained ministers on their own have a decreasing impact even where people perceive their good intentions.

I look forward to the time when we can abandon the terms "shared", "collaborative" or "mutual" ministry. Ministry held in common should be the norm and not something out of the ordinary that needs a special name. The New Testament envisages the church as a body – the Body of Christ (1 Corinthians 12). We need to accept automatically that that ministry belongs to the whole Church, every one of its members. In fact in a growing number of Christian communities there is no ordained minister with whom to collaborate. To use adjectives like "collaborative" is to accept the validity of ministry that is not mutual whereas if the Church is true to itself then there cannot be. Every single member of the Body of Christ is automatically involved in ministry and mission whether or not they perceive it or believe they have opted in for it. People will look at us all, not just the few we think we might have selected, to help them assess if there is anything in Christianity worth pursuing. Every single member (especially those who have belonged a long time) needs to be seen to be authentic – WYSIWYG.

Job Descriptions

I have already mentioned the declining numbers of people offering themselves for ordination. One of the reasons for the decline is that young people do not relate to the old hierarchical model and cannot see themselves working along traditional "vicar-congregation" lines. The minister or priest enables communion, but this need not be for a parish or whole congregation. I have mentioned above the possibilities of employing youth workers who could become ordained "youth chaplains". Both lay and ordained youth workers are vital for the proclamation of the Gospel to younger generations. However, there are many other areas of ministry that could feature in specified job descriptions. We already have hospital and prison chaplains. Chaplaincies in schools could be extended beyond the private sector to include all schools, both primary and secondary, rather than being just another concern that the local minister has to take on. Such persons (lay or ordained) would be specifically trained which will increase the quality of the work. (Currently there are too many parish priests and ministers who are either doing such work under protest or rather poorly, leading to young people perceiving the Church as amateur or uncaring). Other specialist areas could include ministry to older people, industry, commerce, tourists, shoppers – and a plethora of other activities as opportunities or needs arise. Examples of these already exist in some places, but they could become much more common.

At the moment, in most parishes, these possibilities exist but it is entirely the responsibility of the local parishioners, and often the clergy, to resource them. Certainly they are not expected to do it all, but the initiative, the vision and the directing for implementation is expected to rest mainly at the local door without a great deal of back up from diocese or district. One of the ways in which the wider church can assist the local church is to help them formulate job descriptions for their clergy and full-time workers which are not so open ended that too many expectations are raised. Currently few parish ministers have such job descriptions. (If an attempt were to be made to write them for existing incumbents it would reveal just how many different expectations people have of them, and how impossible it is for just one person to fulfil them all.) This does not exclude the continuance of "general practitioners" where such a ministry is felt appropriate, but, nevertheless they too, should have a carefully drawn up job description. Such a specification would exclude general terms such as "running" the parish, or simply being designated "in charge" – responsibilities which belong to the whole communion. The Christian community should be constantly on its guard against giving too much responsibility to any individual, whatever his or her title, because this leads to the dangers, not only of over expectation, but to authoritarianism and "empire building". The local Christian community is not only answerable to God (which should never be forgotten) but is responsible to the wider Church, represented in the first instance by the diocese or district. The concept of a local church independent of the church as a whole is not possible if the Church is the Body of Christ.

Buildings that Reflect Living Church

Most Church congregations are stuck with buildings built in former centuries. They may not be entirely conducive to helping the church to appear relevant. Nevertheless a sense of history is a good thing, so long as the church looks alive and active in the present day. There are things that can be done to enhance the welcoming aspects of the buildings we have inherited.

Let us begin with seating and the general layout of the church building. This has been experimented with since the Second World War with all sorts of new shaped buildings but in so many cases, even in the new buildings, the seating is fixed. It is usually fixed in rows with the people all facing the front where the ministers sit apart and distinct. This is the same week by week. It never changes. In church buildings where everything is screwed down by a society with a non-postmodern worldview in the way they felt things should always be, this speaks of things being solid and heavy and resistant to the freedom of today's world. The answer is to be more flexible. The seating should be rearrangable according to the number present, or for the type of service or event taking place. Sometimes seating will not be needed at all. I am aware of the huge resistance there is to "moving pews" and the vehemence with which those who suggest even a little change in this direction are met. Courage is needed. The advantages of flexible seating to the main Sunday worship are many. It helps with the welcome people receive no matter how old or young and it can be made to incorporate wheelchairs. It is possible to vary it from week to week depending on the type of worship being held. Examples of acts of worship that are designed to be accessible to younger generations today are included in an appendix.

The very fluidity of the world today demands flexibility if we are to fulfil our calling as churches engaged in mission. To those who object that, "most people who belong to this church are happy with it as it is", I would ask the question whether they are content to give the impression that God is static and lifeless. It is not what suits them that matters, it is whether or not they reflect the living, breathing and dynamic God who will set people alight with love and self-giving friendship (John 15:12-14) if they turn to him. A building that is adaptable, free and open speaks far more of the God we know and the God who will connect with people today. The truth is, chairs that can be left a bit untidily make a building feel "lived in", which is often much more attractive than something that is so nice and ordered that people are afraid of touching anything in case they disturb it. A church, no matter how old, should look like a home not a museum, or worse – a mausoleum with all the plaques around the walls. Diocesan Advisory Committees for the care of churches should take all this very much into account. Too often local impetus to really be the church in action is damaged by delay in obtaining the necessary faculties (permission) and people become discouraged. Should the servants of God be seen to proclaim his life-giving spirit, or be servants of preservationists who may have no interest in the Gospel at all? It may be that some congregations will have to leave the ancient building to an historical trust and meet elsewhere. Not a few congregations have already done that.

Worship

Turning our attention to the service itself, the key is variety. Variety does not appeal to those who like the same diet each week. However, it reduces the differences between those who are new and those who have been coming for years. Each is experiencing that same element of exploration. Of course many of the same elements will come up often and people will get to know them but they may be slightly varied and not always present. Sometimes people will gather around the altar, but at other times they may sit facing one another as in monastic choirs or sometimes in small circles. Often they will move around and the layout may change. Small groups could be formed among the congregation during the course of the worship or before it begins. One idea could be to detach the teaching part of the worship from the sacramental part. For example the "service" or "act of worship" could begin as a teaching session in a relaxed atmosphere that allows people to interact with each other and put in their own contributions to a discussion or forum, rather than listen to a sermon with one person doing all the talking. How this could be done would depend on the people present, and any idea could be explored. The congregation could suggest ideas for things for future weeks – so could those who do not yet come to church. Another idea is for people to move around from group to group like at whist drives (not that there is any winning or losing envisaged of course!), or they could go to different corners to pray at different stations or engage in a "labyrinth".[87] For the communion, there could be a deeper meditative atmosphere as people gather around the table, seated or standing, and being especially conscious of being one family in the presence of God. The act of worship could begin or end[88] with people celebrating that fellowship in an informal session around the tea urn which, if possible, should also be in church rather than the church hall. Not only does this prevent people having to transfer to another building in all weathers, it also recognizes the importance of social interaction as part of being church. Some larger churches have fitted cupboards and sinks in side chapels (which can be designed to fit in with the rest of the furniture), others set up tables on one side or at the back.

Those who lead worship have an immense responsibility if the Church is to fulfil its calling in the 21st century. They can make the difference between people recognizing the gift of God to the world, or going away disbelieving and disappointed. The way a service is led indicates the concept of the Church that obtains in a particular community. One which portrays an old fashioned hierarchy with a leader out the front, perhaps on the top step or in a pulpit, who does all the talking is not going to be easy for people from a postmodern background. At some point during worship leaders may be more visible, but not on every occasion or all of the time. God needs to be recognised as our transcendent Lord as well as among us, and we should open out our human circles as we recognize the greatness of God who lives in heaven. Flexible seating allows for this. We should avoid putting human beings in between God and those who come to worship, giving the impression that some people are extra special. They also get in the way of God. Wherever possible we should seek to involve more than one or two people in the leadership of any one act of worship. A service should not be a platform for a "one man" or "one woman" show. Of course a talented or charismatic person may attract quite a crowd, but the point of coming together is not to be entertained, enthralled (or worse, manipulated) by an individual. We come together as the people of God, and that which should be most manifest among us is the presence of God. Far too often leaders dominate worship because they feel they must keep control, even if for all the right reasons. The main problem is not that leaders want to show off (although of course some of them do, and in the process doing the proclamation of the Kingdom a huge disservice) but that they want to know that the service is "going well". Leaders who feel they need to be "in charge" of what's going on tend to say too much – giving instructions as to posture, announcing hymns and page numbers as well as preaching the word and celebrating the sacrament. As a young curate I reckon one of the best acts of worship I was ever involved in leading, was when I had laryngitis!

Sometimes the reason for the same person leading the whole worship is that the planning has been left solely to him or her. It is better that a small group decide on the overall form of the service and then they can invite different people to lead each section. There could be times in the worship for unplanned contributions from the congregation too. We need to trust God and each other and "let it flow" – a fluid way that will be far more meaningful – in which the Holy

Spirit of God can permeate the worship. Sometimes things will go wrong, but no more often than with the "theatrical" type of service which needs to be rehearsed. For the most part worship should be simple and uncomplicated.

The brothers and sisters at Taizé achieve this extremely well. Sitting down the centre no-one is aware of which brother is leading which song or part of worship. The musicians are not visible and people, sitting on the floor facing the east end of the church, look towards a blaze of light, and the representations in stone and cloth of the flames of the Spirit. A brother only becomes the focus of attention when the word is read from the west end, and people turn and face him, or for the eucharistic prayer. This should be our aim in local church worship too. Let us use many voices in the course of a service and allow them to make their own contribution in whatever language or actions come naturally. Young people love to dance, for example, but this need not be "out the front" but in among the people if the seating is arranged to allow it. We should not be afraid of silence, some of which can be spontaneous and not "planned for". In order to facilitate the use of more than one voice we should invest in a flexible microphone system with radio microphones that can be handed around. The world of electronic technology offers all sorts of opportunities for worship such as the projection of images on a screen and the use of every variety of music. This, too, has the advantage of not focusing on individual worship leaders. They both increase flexibility and appeal to young people and children who use them in other walks of life. Worship is a whole lot more meaningful if it is truly shared.

Above all, whatever its nature, whether contemporary or traditional, worship needs to be genuine and sincere (WYSIWYG) and truly God centred – an offering to God that takes us onto a higher plane. If it is not genuine it will have no impact – either on God or people. In fact it will cease to be worship.

Music without Barriers

This brings us to the place music has in worship. In one of her concerts, a benefit concert for world peace in the Cathedral of St. John the Divine, New York, Nana Mouskouri spoke of music as a language that unites:

> Music for me is always a beautiful rainbow with many, many colours. It knows no nationalities, no frontiers, no barriers. It is a language with no barriers because music leads the world, the universe from one end to the other. It leads life, leads the children, leads the future of the world. Music has its own language. It is a language of love, a language of freedom, of dreams and hope, but above all, it is the language of peace.

This expresses the power music has for human beings. It is therefore going to be at the heart of most of our worship. If music is going to be a language of love and freedom in our relationship with God then it needs to be as genuine and sincere as anything we do or say in worship. Music should blend with, and enhance that which we are doing for God. The obvious pitfall here is that music can be an end in itself, and then the whole event becomes a concert. Of course concerts are an important part of life and there is no reason why music should not be performed for its own sake (including religious music), but if it is, then it is not shared worship. Young people love music and they love making it too. They should be allowed to contribute this way, even if what they play, and the quality of the playing, is not what adults would prefer. The guiding principle is that it is done for God. Musicians and choirs should avoid becoming *prime donne,* and allow their worship to be expressed through their music and enabling the whole congregation to be centred on God.

Sadly, music is not always "a language that knows no barriers". Some people relate to one type of music more than another. Some types of music they simply cannot understand. This can result in music being one of the key battle grounds between the generations with different sides deeply entrenched in their views. Emotive words may be used to pour scorn on someone else's preference, and sadly that is more often done by those who are educated in music than by those who just "like what they like". The issue seems to centre around "quality". Quality, however, in the context of worship is to be judged on whether it is a genuine, sincere act of praise or prayer – God orientated and honestly given. If it is, then whether it is made on a guitar, organ, flute or saxophone it has a place in worship in a postmodern world. As many of those present as possible should have a place in it. This may mean that we want to give out copies of the words of hymns and songs, or display them on a screen. Simple repetition is a very good way of involving everybody. For those who think that repetition is simplistic, I would again refer them to Taizé. Even children's music, perhaps with less than half a dozen words, can be meaningful for adults too. "Meaningful" here, of course, signifies meaningful worship. It will not be possible to include everyone's own musical preferences in a single service. Some services will be a combination of different styles of music which may vary from week to week. (This is especially important if it is the main service where we place the emphasis on sharing and communion.) Other services may use one style, a "rock service", for example, or "evensong". The list can be as long as there are people with interest in any style. Postmodern young people have a huge variety of musical taste. "Rock", "indie", "rap", "punk", "pop", "metal", "dance" and "garage" may all be classed as "pop" in the eyes of older people but they are vastly different, and young people have their preferences. As we have already observed, there is a world of choices for young people and they are increasingly diverse. There is a variety of Christian music that is written for young people. They do like this. Songs are often lively and more repetitive and pick up rhythms which are more natural for youngsters. However, it would be wrong to fix on one kind of music and think we have done what's required. Young people change fast and some of the young people's songs we still put on for them were written over twenty years ago (and that makes them "ancient"!). Some of those who lead worship in school are still using the same "contemporary" songs that were used in the 1970s. That might be alright for children but it is a huge put off for young people. When it comes to music for the particular young people in our neighbourhood we must take the lead from them and allow them to make their own music. In fact the young people we have observed who are genuinely worshipping all do this. As soon as older people (and that means anyone over thirty) attempt to do it for them it can cease to be "theirs".

Open Doors

It is essential that everything that Christians do, as individuals and as a fellowship, should be open and abounding in welcome. If Church is about communion – *koinonia* – then worship ought to be the very expression of it. It amazes me just how often church services are so unwelcoming. One French Catholic church we attended recently had no-one at all to greet people and as strangers we had to use our initiative as to what books and papers we would require. We chose somewhere to sit, breathing a sigh of relief after the service had begun to discover we had not sat among the choir, who were placed in a section of the nave. There was no exchange of the "peace", and no joining of hands for the Lord's Prayer (as is common in France). The communion for the people was taken from the tabernacle, and was not part of the bread used at the Eucharist at the mass of which we should have been part. No-one invited us to move forward to receive the communion – in fact there was a rush of people who took no notice of us at all. After the service ended people just left, the priest was nowhere to be seen, and no-one spoke one word to us and very few to each other. There may be fellowship among the members of that congregation, but it was not evident on that day.

Welcome should not only apply as people arrive, but throughout the service and after it too. The responsibility of the people at the door is not just to insure people have the right books but also to make them feel as if they really do belong. Welcoming is not just about words, but body language too. We should look pleased that some-one is there, whether they have been coming for years or just for the first time. We need not worry about this if we are genuinely welcoming. The giving of "the peace" is an expression of the communion we share as we look to God to unite us in the sacrament of communion. When we exchange it we should not only shake hands but look at one another and mean what we say. The French idea of all holding hands as we say the Lord's Prayer acknowledges that we belong together as a family with the same heavenly Father. It has special poignancy when it is placed immediately before receiving the sacrament. The informal gathering around the tea urn in Britain or the *"pot d'acceuil"* in France is also part of the service and the welcome, especially if it is done in the church building. The vital thing about welcome, just as for the rest of the service, is its sincerity. If the welcome is not true, then, not only has the church lost an opportunity for mission, it may have damaged a person's chance of finding God for years. If may have taken a great deal of courage for a person to appear in church for the first time, and the reception they receive is crucial. People who have grown up in church-going can find it hard to understand how difficult it is for people not used to church to enter the building let alone attend worship. "Frightening" is a word often used. When I was a student in a theological college we had a visit from a man who worked in a night shelter for the homeless. One of the students asked, "Do you find it threatening talking to people who are 'down and out'?" "Not half as frightening as coming into this place.", he replied, looking around at the gloomy statues and forbidding portraits of college divines of former years, as well as the group of likely looking students.

We should also be aware of ways to make worship more accessible. To have to go to a church building that has a definite "inside" and "outside" is like attracting customers into a shop with no windows. It is no accident that shop-fronts are 100% windows. In hot lands they even dispense with those. Shops are often open-fronted or simple stalls. Perhaps we could have the doors as wide open as possible in summer weather, or do what some have done, and replace them with plate glass so everyone outside can see right in, even in winter. We might even turn a whole wall into window. It is common for people to hang around in churchyards, perhaps eating sandwiches or just sunbathing, but at the same time listening to what's taking place and exploring if there is anything in this Christianity thing.

By the same token, outdoor worship is essential in all seasons. These can be associated with Christian festivals or just times when people are about. An outdoor nativity in a town centre with a real baby (and perhaps a real donkey) attracts hundreds of people who do not seem to mind singing carols from soggy song sheets. Good Friday and Easter provide opportunities for different sorts of worship. I am amazed at the numbers of people who are prepared to attend an outside Easter sunrise service at six o'clock in the morning, even if there is cloud and cold rain! Seaside resorts can arrange summer season praise services on the seafront. Instead of holding a summer service in church why not have it outside followed by a barbecue instead of tea? Rogationtide in May was traditionally a time for "beating the bounds of the parish" and in some places they are welcomed today in some form or another – not that we should any longer be concerned about fixing impenetrable parish boundaries against either the devil (the traditional idea) or our current neighbour parishioners!

There are those who are far more capable and experienced than I am in designing worship to achieve these aims, but to give an idea of the sort of thing I have in mind, I have drawn up four examples in the appendix at the end of this book.

There are countless examples of ideas in which churches can give expression to *koinonia* and worship God in meaningful, relevant and exciting ways in today's environment at the local level. In truth, despite the rules of the Church,[89] we are restricted only by the limits of our imagination and our honest desire to witness and minister to the God who loves us so much he gave himself to die for us. But in all of this it is important to remember that it has to be genuine fellowship and worship through and through, not just a show. It all has to be WYSIWYG!

9. Spanning the Gulf

In the last chapter we faced the question of finding a way of worshipping that connects with young people today. But this is only part of the challenge. In most places it is already too late to rescue the situation by merely getting the inside activities of church in tune with current culture. The vast majority of young people are not associating with churches at all and do not see themselves worshipping in any way in a church building, no matter how welcoming or radical. Yes, young people are in search of meaning but most of them are unlikely just to drop in on worship in response to an advertisement, or even a personal invitation, for all the cultural reasons described above, including fear of the unknown and the dangers posed by some manifestations of religion. So the onus is on Christians to span the gulf, build the bridges and connect with the young people where they are.

How do we go about this? Where do we begin?

Caring for the Needs of Young People

One the most important things any local church should do is care for those around them. I believe that the most difficult group to do this for is young people. In my team of churches[90] we have over 40 lay ministers of the sacrament taking holy communion to around 130 people who live in nursing or residential homes or are house-bound. We have around 35 people working with children on a regular basis mainly through mid-week groups and holiday clubs. We have 16 lay pastoral assistants but none of them are chiefly engaged in youth work. So who ministers to the young people in our parish? There are two or three very dedicated volunteers (one of them in her seventies) and a full time youth worker sponsored by Churches Together who is everything you can hope for in a person in such a position. But she feels so alone in what she does. Her management group is small and most of the members are not directly involved with young people themselves. She has no team around her and is finding it extremely hard to get one. This is partly because we do not have the people with the skills, partly because the demands of ministry to older people take so much of our time, partly because we do not have young members of our churches with the time or motivation to engage, partly because working with young people is not seen as a priority for our resources, and partly because we simply give it insufficient thought. As well as working with young people, our youth worker is also expected to educate the rest of the church in the importance of youth ministry. She has more than enough to do in one role without adding another. How she manages what she does is a miracle. I believe that is true for many of the youth ministers in our land. I have made the case for the redirecting of resources in chapter seven.

However difficult and under-resourced it is, I believe pastoral care of young people must be at the heart of mission. We must seek to work alongside and within those places young people spend their lives: our schools, universities, youth clubs, festivals, holiday activities, on the street corners and in their homes.

Volunteers can be trained to do this because often in addition to the "professional" attention which needy young people should already be getting, there is a real need for a listening ear and safe befriending. Christian ministers need not be trained social workers – if they feel called to be so, they should undertake all the professional training and obtain all the necessary professional qualifications. The role of the youth minister is to care for the whole person. However experienced we are, we are not teachers, health visitors or social workers – what we offer is a recognition that each person is a child of God, is special, and has ultimate value. When we care we want people to know that we do it not just because we ourselves care (which should be genuine) but because God cares too.

Many schools (church or state) are only too pleased to accept youth ministers to meet with the children. Our secondary schools have immense pastoral care for young people which ranges from problems with bullying through stress and family breakdown, to substance abuse and the truancy that results. Youth ministers can become involved in PHSE (Personal Health and Social Education) lessons and also minister to young people on a "one to one" basis. Youth clubs are always looking for appropriate volunteers. One gentleman in one of our churches served coffee and sweets etc. at the youth club for decades, retiring only months before he died in his mid-seventies. Drop-in centres likewise need ordinary caring people. These places value our support in management, publicity and often fund-raising too. If we are to engage with young people on the streets we need to be really known and as part of a recognized agency for our own safety as well as that of the young people. There is a great need for detached youth workers in our towns and cities and churches should encourage suitable members of their congregations to think about this work. It is important that Christians do this even if the young people do not recognize them as Christians. We should never feel we have let the cause down by not talking about Jesus every time. Our care has to be genuine, centred on the person and without strings. Unless we make our faith a secret someone will recognize the connection and give God the glory.

Musical festivals are very popular with older young people. Not only do they listen to music, there is a tremendous amount of social interaction and debate between people from different parts of the country. Being present at these festivals allows young Christians to share in this interaction. It is important for such young Christians, however, to have a genuine interest in the music and identify with the culture of the people who are there. They have to join in and be part of it. The same goes for sports and sports supporters. It may be difficult at first but they can just let people know what they believe when the time is right. We don't force or lead the conversation, but neither do we duck the truth of our faith when we are challenged. We could seek an official presence at these large festivals. This needs discussing with the organizers but offering a place where young people can chill out would be useful. These ventures need to be properly staffed and properly supported by a number of sponsors. In the biggest festivals these should be inter-denominational.

Ministering to young people within their families is central. Few families manage to avoid some sort of "crisis" in which the children and young people are inevitably caught up. Ministers become involved in caring for the whole family but the young people are often left to sit around on the edges while their parents or the grown ups with whom they live receive the prime attention. Relating to young people in their homes is not an easy process because they are not going to be able to speak freely or want to turn the attention away from the adults in need. Such crises include the death of a relative, a grandparent or great grandparent or favourite uncle or aunt. It could be about caring for a relative that takes a lot of the parents' attention. Occasionally it could be the death or serious illness of a parent or another young person. Increasingly it is about the breakdown of the parents' relationship. A separate youth minister here is extremely useful. It allows the various members of the family to have access to separate care. Even if there is not a specialist youth minister available, ministers dealing with these situations should seek to share the ministry with someone else who is there especially for the youngsters. This makes demands on resources, but if we follow the traditional pattern of a lone minister it is nearly always the case that it is the young people who miss out – no matter how much the minister is aware of it – simply because the adults dominate.

Since speaking to young people in their homes is often not possible, it may be necessary to make arrangements in another place. "Safe" places should be sought within the confines of the child protection guidelines.[91]

Once young people become aware of youth ministers, their genuineness, their honest care, their faith and their availability, the young people themselves will try to make contact. Our experience is that when this happens it is difficult for a single youth minister to meet the demand he or she will receive. The rewards are great because if the minister is able to take the strain and stay the course they will see young people growing through their problems and coming to terms with life and sometimes faith. They will also see them connecting with worship that seems appropriate. It is often not the ones from the most stable homes that respond the most readily, but the ones most desperately in search of meaning and hope. Ministry lies at the heart of our mission. Ministry and mission are two sides of the same coin, and as long young people know that from the outset – so that the whole relationship with them is clear and open from the start – there is a real chance that they will respond to God in their lives. It will not be something we give them, it is something they will discover for themselves. But those in youth ministry will rejoice that they have been instrumental in helping the youngsters along the way.

One of the things that the church has done since the nineteenth century is to provide a safety net for those in the greatest need. Even in our present day when the State provides much more there is still a need to put into place schemes and projects to look after children and young people. Since the Thatcher years there has been a greater emphasis on the voluntary sector. Some of these are national charities and some more local. Some are church sponsored, others by other organizations, and are financed by grants from the Church Urban Fund,[92] for example, and a plethora of other charities. The need for these has not diminished and it is important to ensure that funding and staffing continues.

Pastoral care is something that all young people require no matter how poor or rich, loved or unloved. We need to be imaginative in its provision, open and ready to listen, prepared to share, generous with our time and resources, and 'WYSIWYG' in our intentions.

Enabling Young People to Care

Young people do not always have to be the primary recipients of the attention. In fact some of the most effective ways of getting alongside them is to involve them in care for others. Sometimes this will mean being involved in something the community or church is doing and sometimes it will commit us in supporting them in the projects they choose to pursue. Working in partnership for the needs of the world helps young people to feel appreciated and valued. Indeed, far from being "in the way" young people are, in fact, incredibly important for the quantity and quality of care that we can give.

Two of the church youth groups that I have been involved with have been called "service schemes". The young people had a great time in doing things together but they sought to use their talents to be of service. One group was particularly good at singing and dancing and, with the help of an able musician, put together concerts and entertainment for the church, community and beyond. They had a wonderful time which was all the more meaningful in that it brought so much joy to other people. Another group made a sound and picture slide presentation about an issue in the community that could be shown in other groups ranging from the Mothers' Union to youth clubs elsewhere. (Today they would have probably used more up to date technology). They wanted to draw attention to how it feels when adults neglect their children. The young people wrote the script, acted the parts, took the pictures, and did the commentary. The leaders enabled the process by obtaining the finance and equipment and took the finished product around. The groups that benefited enjoyed the young people and took the issues seriously. This process needed committed adults to find the resources and others to agree to receive the offering. Not all adult groups are open to being challenged by young people telling them what it feels like when they fail in their duty to their children, and the young people's leaders sometimes take a bit of flak. When they do they need to be supported.

As a young person myself (a long time ago), I was part of a scheme that befriended housebound people. We each had some-one to go and see on a regular basis. We went in pairs – "it's nicer in twos" as Winnie the Pooh says, but not just for that reason. (Once again, check your child and vulnerable adults protection policy). We did the garden for her – but mostly sat around drinking tea and eating her chocolate biscuits. That friendship lasted into my early forties because, although the lady was widowed without children and housebound by severe arthritis, she was only in her fifties when we began visiting her. After I went on to university the father of one of the young people did a great deal of caring, sometimes on a daily basis. All of this came out of the thoughtful concern and imagination of our youth leaders. The young people thought they were helping the older people, the older people were doing it for the younger, and the youth leaders were doing it for both. The whole project was sponsored by the church.

Campaigning for a better world should involve young and old together. One World Week, the World Development Movement and Trade Justice help us to witness to what our faith demands of us. It is no accident that it is right at the outset of his ministry that Jesus reads from the book of the prophet Isaiah declaring that he has come to bring good news to the poor. (Luke 4:16f). It sets the tone for all that follows. Isaiah of Jerusalem pleads that religion is a mockery if there is no justice (Isaiah 1:10ff). If young people are going to take Christians seriously then we have to be at the heart of campaigning for righteousness. We need to reflect the demands of our faith if we are to be seen to be genuine. The trouble is that the church comes across as stuffy and detached from real life. If it isn't, then the young people of western Europe need to see that it isn't. If it is, then it is essential that we change it. This is something we should tackle at local levels and national ones.

Young people cannot watch the news of our broken planet without wanting to take action. Where should they begin? The television helps with things like "Children in Need" and "Red Nose Day", but youngsters need adults to help them put together their fund raising ideas. Church members can be part of this process. There are thousands of other charities that children identify with ranging from sponsoring a street child in the third world to supporting the local donkey sanctuary. One woman who reckoned she could not talk to young people because she did not know what to say to them was delighted to discover a common interest in a Christian Aid project. The local Save the Children fund raising committee has young people as committee members. They raise hundred of pounds through a school rag week each year by "insulting" teachers in a rag mag, selling kiss-a-grams and collecting copper coins. All good fun – and the young people get a great satisfaction as well as benefitting the charity.

Most young people have a sincere concern for the world, its peace and the people who suffer. Christianity purports to be a religion of love. After all, Jesus said we would be judged on the care we share with others (Matthew 25:31*f*). There are Christians who find it difficult to advocate the church "giving money (or things) away", claiming that what the church has received should not be spent on anything but its maintenance and immediate ministry. This is a poor witness to young people who believe the church should not just encourage people to support charities independently, but seek to allocate a proportion from their central funds too. If some churches find it difficult to do this they should ask themselves why others are able. Some of our poorer churches give the most generously. This is certainly true of individual Christians. Jesus' observation of the widow and her "mite" (Luke 21:1-3) is as true today as it was in Jesus' day. If the church is to be seen by young people as truly embodying the teachings of Christ, then its practice has to be seen to be more caring than the general community. Young people are inspired by genuine and sacrificial concern and giving, and one of the reasons they reject the church is that it seems to spend a huge amount of money on itself and much less on meeting the needs of the poor. Let us not only seek to inspire our youth but be inspired and challenged by them in return. Partnership in tackling the shortcomings of the world will bring us all nearer to God, the Source of life itself.

Sponsoring Youth Events

Since the second world war in particular, Christians have put on youth events. These have proved universally popular and, despite the young people deserting regular worship in droves, do not seem to have diminished in popularity. Indeed in some instances their popularity appears to have increased. Residential happenings are especially popular. These range from locally organized camps or week-ends, to Greenbelt and the like. Children's holiday clubs (special days from 9 am. till 3 pm.) which are stocked with full-scale biblical teaching are often over-subscribed. This is an indicator that children and young people crave some organized activities in the holidays and parents are only too pleased to let them go. Young people are not averse to getting the Gospel teaching in undiluted ways so long as they know what they are letting themselves in for. Parents are reassured if they are satisfied that the children are not going to be manipulated. All but a few are pleased that the children are hearing words of hope and exploring genuine spiritual expressions of love, peace and joy. So long as the children remain in control of their own choices, and are allowed to respond to the evangelism with a genuinely free heart, most responsible adults seem to be happy for the young people to participate.

Providing these activities is extremely demanding for youth leaders both in time and energy. It is not the absence of young people that limits the work, but the shortage of willing and able leaders. It may be that we need to be imaginative to get around this problem.

Pilgrimages are an enjoyable activity that can be "all age". This is especially valuable if you want to do something to bring a fellowship together that includes worshipping young people. Exchanges are also popular. Why not seek to entertain a number of young people from abroad, or another part of the country, that can be billeted in families? Or get a group together to visit some-one else. Young people delight in meeting other young people from somewhere else. If you have insufficient people to do things yourselves, or even if you have, then think about finding WYSIWYG Christian camps and pilgrimages on which to enrol young people. In addition to that (although it's perhaps more expensive) small numbers of young people can sign up for events and courses at places like Lee Abbey[93] or spend a week at Taizé.

Supporting and Supplementing Religious Study

As we have seen investigating spirituality is increasingly important for young people. They are fascinated by honest inquiry into religion and the things of God. The philosophy of religion and ethics are central to this. They look to us to be informed of faith and to be prepared to discuss and share it with them in a thought out way. "Sound bites" or surface understandings are not sufficient.

One young woman of 19 described to me the bits of the bible about morality as "beautiful". She believed that each person should "internalize" their own ethic. In this way she described certain things she owed to herself and those around her as her "duty". The word "duty" here is subtly different from the usual dictionary meaning of duty which runs "behaviour due to superior, deference, expression of respect" or "moral or legal obligation, what one is bound or ought to do". For her, duty springs from a person's own chosen ethic. It is necessary, she believes, for each person to research, think through, and adopt for himself or herself, the standards by which he or she live their lives. This particular person bases her choices on the primacy of love – for herself (self-respect), her family and for other people. This determines her view of her personal behaviour, her relationships, and her attitude to the world. This is a far cry from "love and do as you like". Sexual relationships are controlled (freedom of choice does not mean "free love"). She honours her parents, and believes in justice for the third world. She rejects elitism, and holds that disaffected people need to be helped rather than outcast. When she looks at the church, with all its history and the authoritative stance it has taken in the past and still appears to take today, she notices "gaping holes" between belief and practice. The church has been, and still is, corrupt (and in some periods of its history extremely so) and its doctrines insensitive. Listening to her, I was reminded of the church as described by Philip Pullman in his *His Dark Materials* trilogy.[94] Nevertheless, there is a role for the church, she believes, and it should remain in being. It needs to be there to support those people who turn to it, to help them know about the promises of God. This is especially important for old people worried about coming to the end of their lives, she thinks. Without the church, she admits, she would not have had the faith in God she has, or the resources to form her own chosen ethic. People also need prayer and to pray. The sad truth is that the church does not measure up to the standards young people hope for. But what is worse is that many people in the church behave as if everything is as it should be, and that the problem is with the young and not with them. They come over as pompous, authoritarian and out of touch. So our 19 year old does not reject the concept of "church" but the church as she sees it. What she wants is church members who are informed and able to help her explore. It is amazing how many young people come forward to ask, if they believe those people are capable, faithful, genuine, informed and not didactic. Unfortunately so many church people fail on the "informed" bit, so if we are to help our young people then we should consider education and formation for adult members too. The church is getting better at this all the time and there are great signs of hope in this direction. The desire to get deeper is not confined to young people.

I have described this personal "testimony" of an individual in some detail because it helps us to form a response. Too often we go about answering the wrong questions. In the past, for example, in the Modernist era, the problem of suffering or the complexities of the Trinity disturbed young minds. Today that is no longer the case. What is important for them is that God honestly cares and is genuinely involved with his creation. Young people do not see that the church, concerned with itself, reflects such a God of love.

We cannot change the past and the church will always have to bear the guilt of its corrupt members – especially when they do bad things today. There is plenty of unseemly behaviour among us all the time. But there are two things, by the grace of God, we can change. First, ourselves now, and, second, the overall thrust of the church in the future. We must pray to be Christ-like, not just in personal behaviour but in our priorities. Then we should be prepared to debate our faith so as to help young people find the resources to form their own ethic, their own internalized *raison d'être,* to discover foundation blocks on which they can base their lives. We should try to introduce them to the bible and help them find the "beautiful bits" (and understand why there are some ugly bits too – and how to cope with them). It is essential to testify to the work of the Spirit in our own lives, and in the lives of those around us.

A further practical consideration is that with such a demand at our schools for religious education courses it is important that we make ourselves available as resources. If we can articulate our beliefs and the reasons we do what we do teachers will use us. Of course they will not call us in if we are going to "preach" in a paternalistic way, but the genuine sharing of something that we have thought through and studied, as well as lived, is valued. It has to be honest of course – including the bits we are struggling with ourselves. But young people respect that and are all too suspicious of things that are too neat and tidy. They do not want things to be easy or simple (because that is bound to be false to some degree) – they want it in all its complexities and loose ends. This demands that we all need to rethink our faith. Just doing things "because we were brought up to it" is no longer good enough for today's young people. But if we have put a modicum of thought into "why" as well as "what" then, like the Athenians in Paul's day (Acts 17:16-34), they want to hear about it. Their journey is a real one, a spiritual pilgrimage, and they want us around to help them decide which way they are going to head. So we have to be there. We need to provide from each of our churches people who are prepared to share the things of faith, and their own Christian journeys, in a demanding and honest environment. At the moment not enough Christians are prepared to do this but it is moving in the right direction.

Consultation and a Willingness to Listen – Letting Young People Back Across the Bridge

Not only is it necessary to share our own journeys, we need, and will profit from, listening to the journeys of our young people. Young people are better equipped at contributing to the debates of our age than we often give them credit for. At school they are taught to access information, marshal their thoughts and come to reasonable conclusions. They are also encouraged to research sources and not to accept other people's opinions as read. This may be frustrating for us if we are people used to getting our way without question. Some may think it is insubordinate. But that is the point. If we are to gain the involvement and trust of young people in our churches and Christian fellowships then we have to give them the opportunities to contribute what they have. In many cases what they can bestow has much value and that sometimes means we have to step back. This comes hard when we have grown up in a culture that has forbidden it. Not only does it go "against the grain", it is also hard to take when we have waited all our lives to get to the "top of the heap", only to be told to listen to "inexperienced youth". But despite their youth, thinking young people are often not only quite well read, they also have experience of a world that is different. Let us, then, consult them and involve them in our decision making and in in our faith journeys.

Bob Jackson in *Hope for the Church* reiterates some of the ideas in which the church could "grow younger". He advocates respecting young people and allowing them to lead by inviting them to join the Parochial Church Council. "If there are older teenagers in the church, at least two should be on the PCC, and their perspectives taken very seriously." (Jackson: 152). Most churches would not be in such a position, but those that are should heed this advice. Experience shows, however, that even the best of PCCs is not very "cool", because the sort of business that they have to discuss is often very dull and of little interest to the younger generation. The worship, or ministry committee is another matter perhaps. But the real consultation comes with young people in larger groups on subjects they are interested in. These are sometimes centred less on the nuts and bolts and more on the principles, policies and premises of what we are doing. They especially want, naturally, to be consulted on the things that concern our ministry to young people, including its resourcing. One comment I once overheard went something like this: "How dare those young people think they can spend our money!", It certainly reveals clearly the unwillingness of that person to allow young people onto his domain. This is a common problem young people have, but it is a problem that can be overcome with imagination and courage on behalf of the people that support them. I was once approached by a group of young people who thanked me for what I had done for them. I was rather taken aback because I hardly knew them and could not recall speaking to any of them much. I could not think what I was being thanked for. It transpired that I had openly disagreed with a woman about her stance on "the problem of teenagers" and "I had stuck up for them". I was working to get them a foothold of recognition as valuable members of the community who have something positive to contribute and it was appreciated.

One very effective way to hear young people's contributions is to allow them to address a meeting from the front on issues that they know something about. On a recent occasion, as part of a day on evangelism, we discussed mission to older people, to those in the working years and to young people. When we got to talking about teenagers, a very brave girl of 15 told an audience of over a hundred people how a new relationship with God had turned her life around. She admitted to suffering extreme problems brought about by very low self-esteem. Although she was a very able girl she had not realized what she was capable of. She constantly under-achieved at school and her relationships were at best unsatisfactory in all parts of her life. Her encounter with a Christian youth worker enabled her to discover a God who could change all that. As she spoke you could have heard a pin drop. What her witness did for those people not only changed their opinions about teenagers, but led us all to travel a bit further on our own spiritual journeys. What she had to say about God was so real that despite her age she had a memorable impact on that audience – both then and since. One of the lessons I learned was that if you want to deal with the issues that confront young people then invite them to speak and to share. Not all youngsters will be able to speak to a meeting of a hundred people, but in groups they will nearly always be prepared to tell a small number of older people how it is. That is why we called ourselves "the listening people" on our fact finding tour. This book could not have been written without the great and generous help of young people who have been so ready to talk to us.

Relationships are always two-way things. If we are seeking to span the gulf that is set between the generations then we should be prepared to allow them to cross back and forth. If we go out of our way to invite young people to consider God then we should not be surprised if young people show interest in the places we come from. When they come, even if only for a fleeting visit, they will leave their mark. I have already mentioned the concern about "spending our money". "Attending our clubs" is also a problem. I am reminded of the remark made by a short mat bowls player who resented the team with enthusiastic teenagers who, he said, "didn't take the sport seriously". I believe it was more a case of them being better bowlers than not taking things seriously. Sadly some people see church as their club. If we are going to take an interest in young people then it will change our fellowships, our finances and our buildings, even if we worship separately. And we have to let them be changed!

Respecting Young People's Space

One thing to note in this process of consultation, is that young people will usually talk more openly and clearly if those they are talking to are not associated with things close to home. If family, or friends of the family, are present they will often be more guarded in what they say. Teenagers, for all sorts of reasons which are perfectly healthy and proper, will feel inhibited in baring their souls to adults among whom they are growing up. This may also apply in some cases to their peers. It is wise, therefore, not to refer back to conversations in different contexts without the explicit permission of the young person or persons. In the process of establishing themselves in the world they are also establishing their own self-esteem and it is very easy to embarrass them. We should seek never to belittle them in their own eyes or the eyes of others (even if we mean no harm). Young people, no matter how articulate or intelligent, forthright or brave, are vulnerable and we should not forget that.

We must be very circumspect when we go out to meet young people. Enthusiastic Christians are often brave. Sometimes they take their courage in their hands and head off to the places where young people hang out to "evangelise" them in a variety of ways, some more subtle than others. I believe this is inappropriate. We need to respect their space. Imagine how adults would feel if people with an "agenda" invited themselves along to a local reception, for instance, and began to gatecrash our conversations. Young people may meet in public places, but that does not mean they do not have a right to some private space. Furthermore we need to be aware that young people under eighteen (and over) are vulnerable to predators who have intentions that are not at all honourable. We have to absorb into our minds an instinct for making their world a place "safe from harm". If we want children and young people to trust our Gospel message then we have to be truly trustworthy. It is not good enough to say that we, ourselves, would never dream of hurting anyone. We have to be aware that other people coming behind us, or even alongside us, may not have the same innocent intentions. It is not wrong that young people turn their backs on strangers, it is what they have been brought up to do. But it is not just strangers that pose the problem, it is often people who have worked at being known over a period of time, and being associated with a church outreach is one way of achieving this. We cannot, therefore, just enter the world of young people without careful preparation, due regard to their safety, and respect for their space.

Christians working with young people, therefore, should never do so on their own initiative and should always work through a recognized agency – statutory or voluntary. Churches who intend to found their own agencies must see that they are recognized by local authorities and work in partnership with existing agencies. It is my view that churches should not set up their own outreach organizations independent of the current providers unless there is no alternative. We should work in partnership wherever possible. Networking is the key, not only to safe practice, but effective practice. There are some very experienced and effective youth workers on our streets who know the needs of the young people in their areas well. They value voluntary support from people willing to train, and we should always work with them whenever possible.

Articulating Our Own Agendas

Before we can engage with young people we need to be able to say exactly what it is we are aiming at. This must be agreed by all those taking part. This is necessary not only to ensure that we remain "on track" and work as a team, but that what we do and what we are saying is consistent with what we are intending. Young people will detect in seconds if we are not WYSIWYG. We need to be up front with young people about where we're coming from, but also what we're aiming at in a particular encounter, meeting or event. Different activities could have different aims. We could, for example, be part of a drive to get a skate park built and if that is the case it should be that and only that. We should have a genuine interest in the skate park, and it would be wrong to associate with the campaign merely to try and persuade young people into our church youth club. On another occasion it could be about telling the Good News of Jesus in a beach mission. In this case it would be wrong to associate with that if our intention is really to get the council to clean up the beach (or, as in one case, to attempt to prevent nude bathing). We should not have "ulterior motives".

This does not mean, of course, that Christians should "hide their lights under bushels". To do that would in itself be dishonest. Young people should know us for what we are, and for what we believe in. There is a world of difference between manipulating people into signing up for our fellowship by inveigling ourselves into their lives, and allowing people to see how we believe our faith changes our life. My intention, as a priest but primarily as a Christian, is to witness to the Kingdom of God. I believe that if I seek the Kingdom of God, all the other things I want for the world, including young people, will follow. In speaking about getting the basic things of life in this world Jesus says, "But strive first for the kingdom of God and his righteousness, and all these things will be given to you as well." (Matthew 6:33). I make no secret of this, but if I am alongside a young person with a drug problem, for example, I am there to help them with that specific need and must do that with all my heart and be properly equipped to do, say and act in ways that tackle the specific problems. I should never open with something along the lines of, "you know that if you came to our church, or if you invited Jesus into your life, you would have help to overcome your troubles". They know I am a Christian. They know I believe that God is at the root of my life. They know I care because I believe God cares. And they know that I believe God helps people in trouble. But they should also know that I am not going to talk about that unless they want to. When a young person is ready they can bring up the subject of faith and they know I won't laugh at them (like some adults or their peers), and I won't begin to force anything on them they don't want. If we help in Christ's name, even though we never mention him, most young people will automatically make the connections and give God the thanks for anything they receive from us.

Making the Most of the Teenage Years

If there are those who are still saying that that is all well and good but they still do not know where to begin, I would urge them to continue to use their imaginations and to pray. It is not good enough to say that we've thought about it but we've decided to leave the question of reaching young people to others. For example, if we decide we are not going to be at the "coal face" (and not all of us are called to be) then in what way are we going to provide the back up and resources to forward this urgent task?

The stages of our childhood and teenage years come and go in no time. There is some trauma to this, but there are also great delights and great experiences. When we are teenagers we have many things and emotions that we experience for the first time which can be absolutely delightful. There are other things that are disasters. Whether they are delights or disasters often depends on the people around us, the people we live with and those with whom we play.

We cannot re-live our teenage years. We cannot come back to the things we never really completed, or for which we needed help when there was no-one around. As an adult we can. (When I retire, I promise myself, I shall grow fuschias. Now I have cherished this for at least fifteen years. Whether or not I ever get round to it is yet to be seen, but it can wait and I could get just as much joy out of it at 65 as at 40.) But I cannot go back and fill in the gaps from my teenage years. What happened then was vitally significant for the rest of my days and had to be done in that period of my life.

Neither can I go back and do those things with my children that I wish I had done when they were teenagers. The promises of attention, when I assured them I would be there "sometime", and that "sometime" never came to be are numerous. The unfinished model aeroplane and the book we were reading that was never completed remain to remind me of the myriad of other things that I never delivered on. The lives of the teenagers in our families and in our neighbourhoods are all equally short and equally important. One of the reasons I never got round to things is that I was always so busy. As I observed above, when talking about pastoral care for young people, adults demand the prime attention. They often get there first, both because they claim prior status, and because they are more practised at getting what they want. The most vulnerable are left behind. The adults are also the ones who can pay. Their need may be immediate, even desperate, but the need to spend time and care among teenagers can make the difference to a lifetime of delight or pain.

I fear the church has let young people down for a long time in terms of the degree of time, attention and resources it invests in them. It is not just a change in culture in a postmodern age that is to blame for the shrinking of the church, it is to do with our failure to put in enough care to the young. This is not only the church of course, it is true of society as a whole where people are bent on their own material gain or obtaining a piece of the action for themselves – or simply want to be left to their own devices unbothered by young people.

It is an indictment of our society that we consider the teenage "problem" as not a problem primarily for the teenagers but for us. In a recent church housing project for local young people who were homeless and jobless, I was told by some vociferous people that they did not want young people near them. They had formed an impression of young people as noisy, drunk and "high" most of the time and the best thing for them was to leave the town altogether. The local member of parliament was brought in, and I received a number of hurtful letters claiming I did not care for old people and that the project was "dirty". Some of these were unrepeatable. A campaign was launched that frightened older residents and a local councillor declared that the area was becoming a "dustbin" for disaffected teenagers – a statement that gave rise to the newspaper headline: "Dustbin Dorset".[95] I found the whole process personally distressing – what it felt like to the young people thus labelled I can only begin to imagine! Several years have passed since then and there are now a number of happily housed young people that the housing association not only trained in building on the job and in gaining NVQs, but found permanent jobs for afterwards.

One of the things, of course, that lies behind this sort of rejection is fear of change. Many older people, and those for whom this world is a present source of material prosperity, are worried about themselves and their society. They read the papers and watch the television and are beset by waves of a sense of insecurity. The church with its historical buildings and ancient traditions can seem like the last safe place and they believe traditions, being the perceived gift of God, should be held sacrosanct and immutable to be held up as a defence against cultural innovations. The young and those who seek change are seen as rejecting these traditions. But in reality tradition and change are not opposed. Tradition informs change but does not seek to prevent it. Indeed at the heart of Christian tradition is growth and development, inclusion and out-reach. In her book *Transforming Practice*, Elaine Graham debates the inclusion of feminist theology into Christian practice. She argues: "Tradition is seen as alive and organic, to be reappropriated in the pursuit of *praxis*. The role of tradition is thus to be indicative, but not definitive ... Interpretation of tradition is forever open and eschatological in focus, because its validating focus is embodied, situated and purposeful practice." (Graham : 198-199). In arranging postmodern alternative worship, Jonny Baker declares: "One of the distinctive features of alt. worship has been a revival of interest in the worship traditions of the church." (Baker, xiv). Most young people do not want to "bin" the riches of tradition, but neither do they want to be confronted by people who use tradition to oppose them.

As a society, and especially as representatives of the Kingdom of God on Earth, we cannot ignore the demands on us to accept and work within our changing society, not least for the sake of our young people. We have a very short time in which to help them establish enjoyable, meaningful and worthwhile lives undergirded by hope and faith. I am the happy person that I am because, among other things, I met some very great people – church people – in my teenage years. Some of these were fellow young people. The most important, however, were the adults who put in place the structures, the teaching and the love that made it all possible. I was a fortunate teenager. My hope and prayer is that teenagers today in this challenging world may be able to encounter people who are equally caring. There is no time to lose!

10. Indicators of Success

How do we measure success in effectiveness in passing on the Good News to young people? This is a vital question because it determines what happens next. If we make a positive evaluation of something then we are likely to repeat it or build on it. If there is no apparent success then we may abandon something, or at least heavily modify it. The measure of it is often, therefore, the cause of much heated debate.

Our difficulty in a fluid world is that it is incredibly difficult to "see" what we have done or what we are achieving, especially in people's hearts. Traditionally success for the church has been measured in numbers attending services, or signed up on church rolls. Pete Ward points this out very clearly in a section headed, "Attendance at Church Services Equals Faithfulness":

> In the game show The Weakest Link contestants are asked questions in turn. A correct answer gives a certain amount of money to the individual, but this money must be banked if it is to form part of the eventual prize. Solid church has its eyes firmly on the bank. The local church may support many good and important activities, including mission trips, evangelism, youth ministry, social projects, and so on, but they are all assessed in terms of their effect or otherwise on regular Sunday attendance. People may have turned to Christ through the youth mission or Alpha course, and this is good, but if they are not banked, they don't really count, until they start to attend Sunday services. (Ward, 17)

Clearly, for all the reasons we have encountered in our exploration of a postmodern liquid world, just seeing whether people are in church on a Sunday is not going to be enough. A youth leader despaired that despite attracting the young people that came to a midweek Christian group she could not get them into church on Sundays. She felt a degree of failure because Sunday church goers could not see much for her efforts. The work wasn't "banked". On the other hand an honest priest in another parish expressed concern that the young people who came to church every Sunday to sing in the choir could not be attracted to join any activity involving exploring their faith. Nevertheless, when the bishop comes, the congregation can boast about their young people! What we need to measure, if we are going to do anything meaningful at all, is people's relationship with God. How far have they entered into the Kingdom of God? We all know people who might be regular church attenders for whom God means very little. They go out of habit, for the music, because they are made to go by their parents or because they want to meet one of the boys on the back row, and a myriad of other reasons.

But these all get counted. The people that go out into the park and sit and pray, or perhaps talk to God in their hearts as they do the washing up, are not on any church's list. There are students who know more about religion and the search for God than many a member of a Church Council, but because they are never seen "in church" their quest is not recorded. In the course of life we encounter many people who live in the Spirit who will never be numbered in any human book, but who may very well be in "the Lamb's book of life" (Revelation 21.27).

We need to include a note of encouragement for those local churches and their leaders who might be tempted to lose heart. What we do may not bear visible fruit this year or even next, or in our part of this fluid world. The impact of Christian witness is cumulative. Some places may be privileged to reap the benefits of years of faithful witness that have taken place elsewhere. Their churches may be humming, but they should have the humility to recognize that it cannot be all their own work. Others should not lose heart because their own efforts do not appear to sustain "good numbers". Indeed, a rise in numbers may be indicative of something other than faithful witness. If filling churches is the end objective of the game then we can do that by using all sorts of attractive gimmicks and personalities which have nothing to do with the Gospel. Bob Jackson comments, "Churches that major on 'church growth' are often driven communities with a tendency to get people in and then to use them, perhaps as fodder for empire building. Furthermore, playing the numbers game in a very focused way often does not result in much numerical growth." (Jackson, 23).

In saying this I do not wish to give the impression that I do not believe coming together is central to what it means to be a Christian. It is vitally important for young people to attend our churches. As we saw in chapter seven, communion and fellowship are indispensable. The point I am making here is that counting "bums on seats" is not in itself a meaningful way of evaluating whether or not we are getting the good news of the Kingdom across – to young or old.

Is there, then, any effective measure that we can bring to bear to evaluate our work as Christians? There is, in the end, only one way of assessing an individual's faithfulness and that is through the works they perform. Jesus tells us that we will recognise the faithful by their fruits. (Matthew 7.16). St. Paul emphasises that those who live in the Spirit display the fruits of the Spirit: "love, joy, peace, patience, kindness, generosity, faithfulness, gentleness, and self-control" (Galatians 5.22). Little of this is about countable numbers. I would like to suggest eight ways that we should use as indicators of whether we are on the right track in today's supermarket world.

***1)* Outreach and Proclamation.**

The first is whether or not we have made the Christian faith available in the section labelled "spirituality". Are we as a local church conscious of ensuring that is so in our area? Clearly we are not alone in this. There are other congregations and individuals too who are "in the market", but what counts is not whether we are there to gain members but whether we are there to invite people to try the things of God, and that is something we can probably do more effectively together.

***2)* Welcome.**

Secondly, how good are we at welcoming and being open to inquirers? In a supermarket there are assistants engaged in stacking the shelves who are trained to be helpful if someone wants some guidance about the whereabouts or nature of a product. Are we available to be asked, and when we are, do we greet people with a smile and treat them as folk who matter, or are we like the grumpy shop assistant who sighs heavily because he does not want to be disturbed?

***3)* Growing into God.**

Thirdly, are we prepared to grow ourselves? How much do we dip into the supermarket offerings? How much learning and formation is going on in the Christian fellowship, as individuals and in groups? Are we open to exploring new possibilities and travelling deeper into God? How ready are we to use our imagination and experiment spiritually?

***4)* Experiment and Adaptability in Worship.**

How ready are we to explore new ways of worshipping God? Successful artists and musicians are always developing their art. Scientists are always seeking to know more and the best ones are ready to be truly adventurous. Whether we are new to faith, teetering on the edges or long in the tooth we should be ready to try out new things, and learn from people who may be much younger than ourselves.

***5)* Participating in Communion.**

This requires coming together in faith. It is much more than bums on pews on Sunday, although Sunday worship, especially the sacrament of Holy Communion, is the central activity. The key word is 'participating'. It involves hearts and minds as well as posteriors! An indicator of this is how much involvement we have in weekday activities and fellowship study and prayer times. How much do we engage in outreach or ministry with others? If we are to "participate in God" (as Paul Fiddes explains) then we participate with each other. "We who are many are one body, for we all partake of the one bread." (1 Corinthians 10.17).

***6)* God talk.**

How well are we communicating? A good test for how often we are engaging in conversations about the ultimate things of life (life, the universe and everything) is whether people are stopping us and asking questions. We will need, of course, to be knowledgable about our faith, but in the final analysis, it isn't about chapter and verse, or who did what in church history, it's about why we believe and how we relate that to things that disturb people – the problem of suffering, moral issues, life after death, how do we know God is there, how do we sort out so many different ideas about God around the world, and so on. There are a lot of books on the subjects which might be good to read, but, in the end, ordinary people want to know how ordinary Christians living in similar circumstances express their faith. If people are not asking questions is it because we are putting them off? Let's take courage and be prepared to talk. This is not the same thing as being pushy, or always going on about God – the sort of thing that gets people's backs up – but simply being prepared to answer questions when asked. Once people know us, they will come to us. Is this happening to people in our own church? One of the important things in relation to young people is whether the local schools or youth clubs are inviting us in to talk to the youngsters. I remember one teacher who, after I had answered a couple of questions posed by some nine year olds, had to be restrained from asking all the questions herself. Apparently my answer to the question, "Who made God?" (which she had thought unanswerable for children) had so intrigued her that she wanted to know if I could answer other seeming imponderables.[96]

7) Caring.

How concerned are we to address people's needs – both immediate and in the longer term? A true church is one which responds to the weakest people in society, people who will probably never manage to get to church or contribute to it because they are too ill, too old or too socially or spiritually incapacitated (Luke 14:13-14). This will involve the giving of time, attention, prayer and money. Often these things will be done in a low profile way – Jesus' principle of not letting the right hand know what the left is doing in this regard is a good one (Matthew 6:3). Sometimes individual Christians will be involved in organizations or schemes that are not church based or church run. The temptation to set up our own church programmes to impress ourselves or others should be avoided!

8) Openness and Honesty.

And, finally, how honest are we being? Does what we do fit what we say? Do we "practice what we preach"? How genuine is our wish to follow Christ and to worship God? Do we really care about other people's circumstances? Are we genuinely wanting people to find God? Are we being honest about the fact that we cannot know everything that is to be known about God, even in this world? Some dare not admit that faith raises challenges for them. That is not something that we need to worry about in a postmodern climate; indeed to admit we are seekers and not people that believe blindly will recommend us to fellow travellers. It will also enable us to receive from others. Nor should we be afraid or diffident about openly rejoicing in the faith we have, or underestimate the value of God's spiritual contribution to the world through us. We should aim to be one hundred percent truthful. What we say should correlate with what we do – "actions", they say, "speak louder than words". Let us not underestimate the power of younger generations to see through pretence (they are educated to be "canny" as they say in the North East). The media is looking to expose every misdemeanour and inconsistency, and our credibility is constantly undermined by long memories of unkind remarks made by thoughtless individual church members, perhaps decades ago.[97] In a local church every one of its individual members must be absolutely WYSIWYG if it is to play its full part in handing on the the Good News of God in today's world. Genuineness is the key. Our aim is not to compete with propaganda, nor just to "fill our church buildings", but to be authentic witnesses of the presence of God in our lives – to proclaim the Kingdom of God. St. Paul speaks of his own mission at the very beginning of the Christian era, a mission we too, can share in the third millennium:

"... as servants of God we have commended ourselves in every way: through great endurance, in afflictions, hardships, calamities, beatings, imprisonments, riots, labours, sleepless nights, hunger; by purity, knowledge, patience, kindness, holiness of spirit, genuine love, truthful speech, and the power of God ..." (2 Corinthians 6:4-7).

With God's help it is possible to be all of these things in all parts of our world – the difficult and challenging corners as well as in those areas where church-going is more popular. Communities which more naturally "congregate" will probably always record the greatest numbers – but a successful church is one that dares follow Christ into less comfortable territory, witnessing to a living hope that is great beyond measuring. One of the more formidable zones is that inhabited by younger generations. Sometimes connecting with youngsters in their trying teenage years can feel a thankless task. Traditionally those who work with young people have been treated as second class and sometimes accused of failing to impose discipline and being responsible for not converting young people to received expressions of church. This must change. I speak after decades of battering by individuals, clergy and church councils concerned with order, noise, keeping buildings looking new, not disturbing neighbours and ensuring worship is decently done. I have always tried to be patient, polite and understanding but, I hope, I will never give in! Too many good people working with youngsters have done so. It can be a very lonely road for them as they struggle with the demands of young people *and* the criticism of adults. Christian youth workers need all the support we can give them. They should never be left to fend alone. It is the responsibility of us all, at every level, to try and understand the world which our young people inhabit and to pray for, support, understand and resource our sharing of the good news of Jesus Christ.

At the installation of a new parish priest in the Church of England the congregation is reminded that the responsibility for mission and ministry belongs to the whole church. The archdeacon asks:

"The church is called in the strength of the Risen Christ to continue his work in the world. Every member of the church is to bring the light of faith to a dark world, to kindle the fire of love in a cold world, and to open the door of hope in a tired world. Will you strive constantly by prayer, word and action, to do all these things?"

And the people respond: "With the help of God, we will"![98]

Appendix: Examples of Interactive Worship

The examples here are included to indicate the way worship is developing. There is a growing number of alternative worship resources coming on the market such as *Alternative Worship* by Jonny Baker and Doug Gay with Jenny Brown. In the introduction they write: "Making alternative worship (and attending it) has been an unwitting crash course in post-modern hermeneutics for many people – they have been asking and answering deep theological questions with their eyes and their bodies." (Baker, xvi).

The acts of worship they follow are all designed to be interactive, incorporate a lot of movement and only occasional central presentation. Worship leaders do not have a high profile, interaction is primarily directed towards God and then to other participants within that God-ward attention.

Ideally each act of worship requires one "facilitator" to every ten participants. Facilitators should be chosen from participants who know what is about to happen and should be representative of all ages, genders and cultures present. Newcomers should be welcomed and then attended to by the same facilitator throughout the worship if they need attention. Care, however, should be taken not to crowd them or make them feel uncomfortable. The aim is to make their introduction easier. If there is to be a "collection" it should be done without "passing the plate" which is always difficult for newcomers. No two acts of worship need follow the same order – even if they contain similar material. This is something different and difficult especially in the mainstream churches where the "order" and "pattern" of worship is meant to be the same even where the content differs. This is what makes an act of worship "formal" or "informal" in the eyes of postmodern generations. Those who are used to the same prayers each week (as, say, in the Book of Common Prayer) regard services in which the sermon is not preached from the pulpit, or in which communion is administered standing in a circle, or where children are invited forward to do a playlet, for example as rather informal. In today's world anything structured in a set pattern is highly formal. Under this definition the sort of "family" or "all-age worship" that we have attempted for the past thirty years is therefore formal. Such formally structured services are important because they root us firmly in Christian worship going back two millennia. However, they are often very difficult for young people to understand and be part of today. In formal services we speak of "congregations", in interactive services we refer to "participants".

In the examples below three of the acts of worship begin with refreshments. This enables people to come in and relax and meet the folk with whom they are going to interact before they enter into worship. It also allows for a flexible time of arrival. (If this seems strange for worship reflect on what happens in the world of work. Business conferences or meetings generally begin with coffee.)

The acts of worship in these examples all demand open space. Pews and chairs should all be moved according to the plans below if at all possible. Sitting in rows does not work for interactive participation. Many schools have long ago abandoned desks in formal rows. Ranks of seats are normally for spectators not participants. Some buildings are more difficult than others but it is possible to adapt interactive worship to the space you have. The plans below presuppose an open rectangular space but if you have pillars or side chapels, for example, with imagination these can be used to advantage.

Planning for these acts of worship is best done by a small group who can allocate various aspects of the service to individuals to prepare. If everything is left to one or two people then not only do those people become over taxed but the variety suffers. Participation begins before the people come together.

In the same spirit many of the ideas below are gleaned from a number of sources to which I am most grateful. I do not claim to be an expert but an advocate. Like a lot of people of my generation I am on a steep learning curve.

Example 1. Theme: Prayer and Worship

1. As people arrive they are greeted at the door by the facilitators/sidespersons and invited to share in refreshments from one corner of the church. (Some churches have specially equipped refreshment areas).
2. During refreshments the facilitators distribute a plan of the church with simple written instructions on it. The theme is explained. They are told they can move into worship when the music begins.
3. After fifteen minutes gentle worship music is played, ideally through a sound system. It is meant to be background and be present in all corners of the church equally. Taizé music is ideal, as are quiet Celtic songs or meditative hymns. The aim is to invoke a "praying" atmosphere.
4. The participants start at any of the prayer stations and move on whenever they feel ready. What is presented at each station will vary according to the local situation – people's expertise, availability of materials, logistics of space, what a particular church has done before etc. Flexibility is part of the exercise. We need to be open to opportunities that present themselves and use them.

   In the example here the stations are arranged as follows:

Praying Stories from The Bible: Posters are displayed with the title "Praying is ...

WELCOME TO St. WHATSIT'S, SOMEWHERE

The theme of our worship today is: **Prayer**

Seats | Seats | Altar | Seats | Children's play area

Seats | Seats

Seats | Seats

Seats | Seats

Table | Door

Praying without words

- At each of the stations around the church you will find suggestions about the different kinds of prayer that Christians have used in the past and use still today.
- As you arrive at a station take in or read the things you see. Think about them. Think about God in silence. If you are with someone else then you can talk to them quietly about what you feel. Stay at each station as long as you like.
- If young children become restless do use the play area with suitable toys.
- We will sing the hymn on the back of this sheet as you move round.
- Later on you will be invited to sit in front by the altar for a prayer and bible reading. Collect a stone or some beads from the table in the centre. You may take these home.
- Feel free to use any seats whenever you wish.

Praying stories from the Bible

Prayers for the needs of the world

The Lord's Prayer

Refreshments

Our Prayer Day

Seats | Seats

PTO for the words of the hymns and readings.

followed by a verse from the Bible. E.g. praying is rejoicing in God (1 Thessalonians 5:16,17,18); praying is sitting quietly with God (Acts 10;9); praying is letting God in (Rev. 3:20); praying is entering into a conversation with God (Romans 8:26); prayer is bringing our needs before God (James 5:13); prayer is bringing other people's needs before God (Ephesians 3:16) etc. Place cards with pictures and stories in paraphrase in language suitable for different ages (lamination is a good idea). E.g. Hannah praying for the gift of a child (1 Samuel 1), Jesus in the Garden of Gethsemane (Luke 22), the Disciples in the Upper Room before Pentecost (Acts 1), St. Peter on the roof-top (Acts 10), Mary the Mother of Jesus in her meeting with Elizabeth (Luke 1), Jesus going up the mountains to pray (Matthew 14:23 etc.), the parable of the widow and the unjust judge (Luke 18), the pharisee and the tax collector (Luke 18), Daniel praying three times a day (Daniel 6) etc. Several bibles with markers in the right places are placed around too. (It is important that people should handle the whole book and get to know where abouts in it they can find a particular reference or story).

The Lord's Prayer: Poster with the words, "Jesus' Kingdom Prayer" and underneath the slogan "God rules, OK!" and "Thy Kingdom Come!" Four trays are put on separate low tables, or the floor, each with a jigsaw. One jigsaw, of no more than eight pieces, is a picture of Jesus teaching his disciples to pray. Another has a jigsaw of six pieces of the text of the Lord's Prayer. The third jigsaw is the same but with more pieces and the fourth has each line of the Lord's Prayer on a separate piece with the challenge to put them in the right order. There could also be a card with the Lord's Prayer printed in three versions – Traditional English, Modern English and New Testament Greek – with a note saying that all our English translations come from the New Testament and written in Greek, but that Jesus probably taught his disciples in Aramaic. People are asked to identify which Greek word they think is the one for "Kingdom", etc.

Our Prayer Day: A display board is placed with the headings: "Getting Up Prayers", "Meal Prayers", "Praying 'As You Go' Prayers" and "Bedtime Prayers". A pile of paper (in different colours perhaps for decorative fun) and pens is placed beside the board. People are invited to write a prayer for one or more category and pin it to the board in the appropriate place. Children could draw a suitable picture.

Prayers for the Needs of the World: A leafless branch with lots of small twigs is set up as a small "tree". Pieces of green and yellow paper in the shape of leaves, and pens are provided and people are invited to write their petitions on the "leaves". The green leaves are for people and situations they know personally and will come into contact with, and the yellow leaves are for situations they have seen on the news – nationally and internationally. As the people hang the leaves on the tree, they offer their prayers in silence. Behind the tree posters from Christian

Aid and other relief charities etc. can be displayed.

An alternative to this is to lay a large map of the world on the floor for people to put pins into the part of the world they are praying for.

Praying Without Words: A large poster is pinned up with the title "Prayer comes from the Heart". Here there is a net on which people can tie pieces of cloth, votive candles to light (keep the candle stand well apart from the net!), incense sticks to light and place in holders or a few incense grains to drop onto lighted charcoal. A pool of water (child's paddling pool?) is placed on the floor. Paper and instructions for origami boats which can be launched are provided. An alternative is floating candles – but not in the same pool as the paper boats. For this station responsible people need to be on hand to ensure that people are safe. Prayer stools can be placed around this area and/or mats/kneelers spread for people to sit/kneel on. Space will determine how much can be done at this station.

5. When most people are about half way round the stations, participants are invited to stand where they are and join in with the first hymn. The hymn should be about prayer or a praying hymn. Ideally it should be well known and relatively easy to sing. The aim is to complement the activities, not detract from them. Singing together allows the people to remember that togetherness is part of being/doing church.
6. When participants are ready invite them to come around the altar. Ensure that older people have preference for the seats (some of them will already be sitting). Invite folk to take a stone, pebble or beads from the table in the centre. When everyone is assembled someone reads (using the sound/loop system) Matthew 6:7-13 followed after a pause by someone else reading Matthew 7:7-11. (If there is room these readings can be printed on the paper with the hymns.)
7. A Collect is said and the people join in the Lord's Prayer and join hands for the Grace.
8. The second hymn is sung. This should be upbeat – a praise hymn. In some churches where everyone knows the *Gloria in Excelsis* this is also appropriate here – but do not introduce it if there are a significant number who do not know it. (Participation is the key and it is important not to lose it at this stage).
9. A blessing is pronounced and the people are dismissed. Include the words and any responses on the hymn sheet.
10. As people leave give them a book mark with a "prayer design" and information about other activities and the date of the next interactive act of worship.

Example 2. Theme: Baptism and the Christian Journey

This service is appropriate for an actual baptism of a child or an adult or simply for the renewal of baptismal promises in, for example, the Easter season. For the purposes of this example we will assume there is a child to be baptised.

A labyrinth is outlined on the floor with masking tape. (See Baker, *Alternative Worship,* Page 26ff.) This is primarily symbolic so need not be too complicated. Labyrinths have been used by Christians for worship, and meditation from early times. They differ from a maze in that there are no dead-ends. Christians, however, have to take great care in life, which is not a labyrinth but a maze. God has given us freewill – but in the example of Christ a "Way" to follow that we need to have with us at all times.

1. For this service the refreshments come at the end because they symbolise the eternal banquet. This is explained as the people are welcomed, given their plan/service sheets and ushered to the west end to stand/sit around the Easter Candle and the Music Group which is playing upbeat Christian songs/hymns which are either projected on a screen above the group and/or printed on the reverse of the plans.
2. When all are assembled the celebrant stands beside the Easter Candle with the child to be baptised and his/her parents and invites every one to gather round.
3. A lay person reads 1 John 1:3, "we declare to you what we have seen and heard so that you also may have fellowship with us; and truly our fellowship is with the Father and with his Son Jesus Christ."
4. The Easter Candle is lit while someone else reads John 1:4-5, "in him was life, and the life was the light of all people. The light shines in the darkness, and the darkness did not overcome it." and after a pause John 8:12, "Jesus said: I am the light of the world. Whoever follows me will never walk in darkness but will have the light of life."
5. The Order of Baptism (which the people have on cards) is used for the section involving the promises to turn to Christ etc. by the parents and godparents concluding with the signing of the cross.
6. A suitable short hymn is sung.
7. The celebrant takes the baptism group to the font and all gather round. The water is blessed, the creed said, and the baptism of the child conducted.
8. Another suitable short hymn is sung.
9. The celebrant takes the child just baptised to the entrance of the labyrinth. Here he/she or probably someone else explains the significance of the Christian

WELCOME TO St. WHATSIT'S, SOMEWHERE

The theme of our worship today is: **Baptism (Christening) and the Christian Journey**

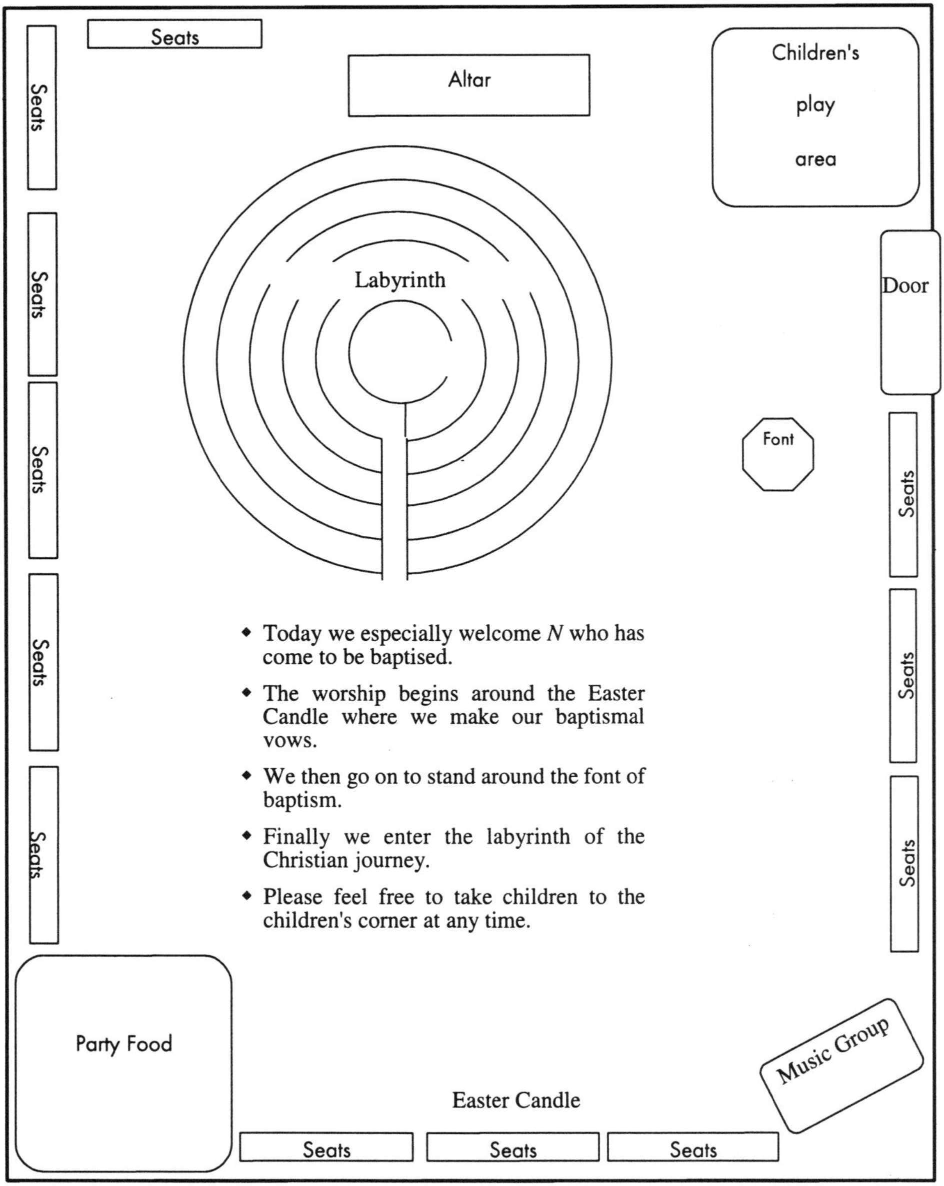

- Today we especially welcome *N* who has come to be baptised.
- The worship begins around the Easter Candle where we make our baptismal vows.
- We then go on to stand around the font of baptism.
- Finally we enter the labyrinth of the Christian journey.
- Please feel free to take children to the children's corner at any time.

PTO for the words of the hymns and readings

journey, the difficulties we are bound to encounter and the power of the Holy Spirit to help us overcome them.[99]

10. The parents and godparents offer prayers. The Lord's Prayer is said.

11. The child is received into the church as the people make the response: "We welcome you". The "peace" is shared.

12. The celebrant explains that the heavenly banquet is promised to everyone who remains faithful to the Christian journey. He/she then invites people to participate in the "party", a reminder of the heavenly banquet, for the newly baptised.

13. The music group plays suitable music as people share the food.

14. Before the family depart the celebrant lights a small candle from the Easter Candle and presents it to the child saying: "Go in the light and peace of Christ! May you travel well on your Christian journey. Remember, as a member of the family of God you always have a home in this place or any place of worship." Certificates are given to the baptised and his/her godparents.

Example 3. Theme: Living the Jesus Way

This is especially suitable for young children but can be adapted to older generations.

1. People are greeted and invited to share in the refreshments.

2. When we are ready the first song/hymn is announced and the people sing it where they are. As music plays they are invited to sit/stand in the central section of the church where the seats have been arranged facing inwards.

3. The people are greeted in God's name and prayers of penitence are said.

4. An appropriate collect is said and the story of Mary and Martha (Luke 10:38-42) is read.

5. An interactive presentation on the story of Mary and Martha is made in which it is emphasised that both are serving in their separate ways but it is always important to stop and listen to Jesus to ensure we are living the Christian way. The presentation finishes with the simple song *"Caring, Sharing"* (from *Big Blue Planet)* 100 to include the very youngest children.

6. Mary and Martha and Jesus' disciple's lived the "Jesus way". The people are invited to think of people they care about and want to share with. They should think not only of their friends but people who maybe they don't like. They should also think of people they have never met but have heard about. We bring all these people together in our minds and think about God looking

WELCOME TO St. WHATSIT'S, SOMEWHERE

The theme of our worship today is: **Living the Jesus Way**

- We begin with informal refreshments.
- There will be time to visit the prayer stations in the course of the worship.
- Please feel free to take children to the children's corner at any time.

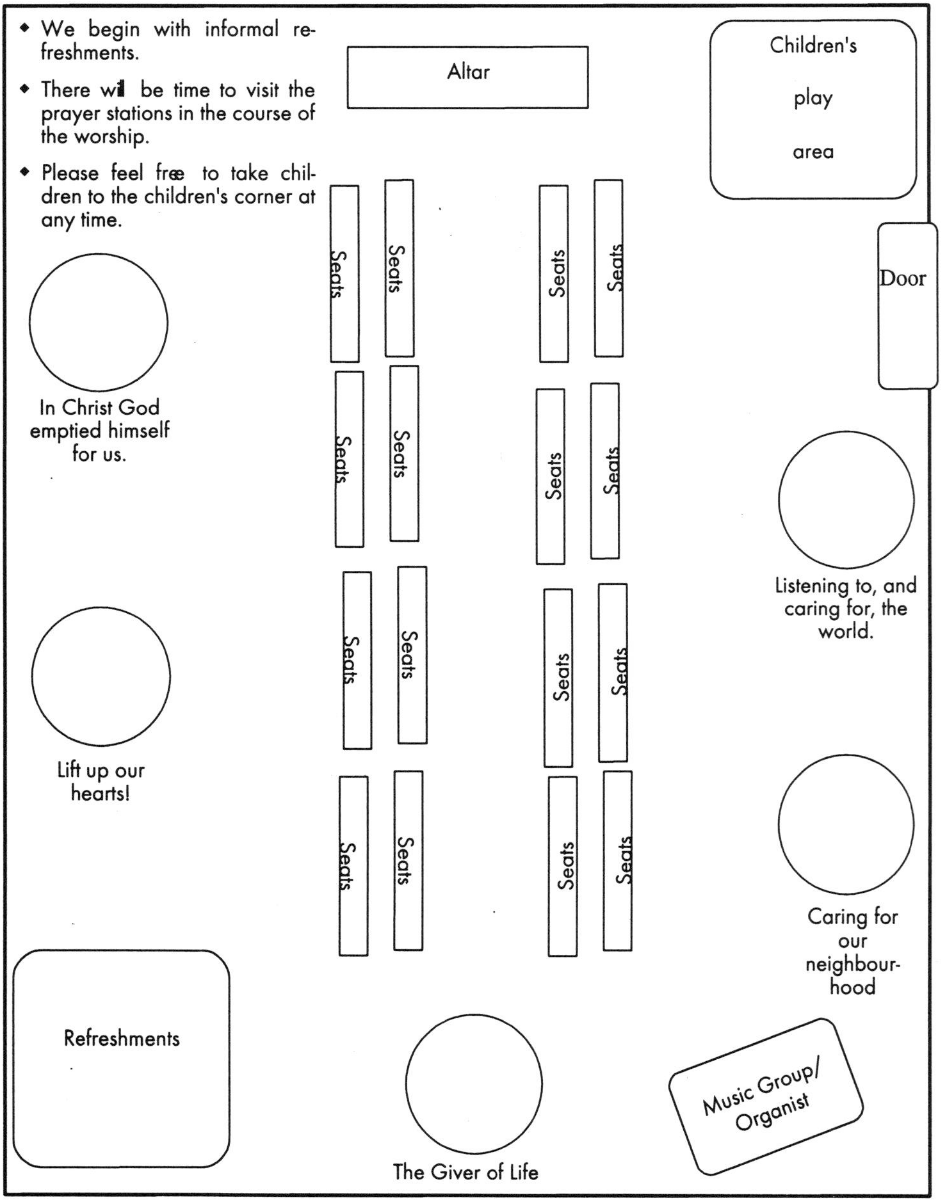

PTO for the words of the hymns and readings

after them.

7. The participants are invited to move around the church to the prayer stations keeping these people in their minds. Quiet, prayerful music is played through the sound system.

Listening to and Caring for the World: Participants put pins into a map of the world mounted on a board. They think about the people in the places in which they have placed the pins. These can range from Uncle Jim in Sydney to street children in Zambia for example.

Caring for our Neighbourhood: A large map (2 meters square?) of the neighbourhood is laid on the floor. A low candle is set up and lit beside the map together with a pile of "tea-lights". These are lit from the low candle and placed on the map in the place where the people we have in mind either live or relate to.

The Giver of Life: A large glass bowl is placed in the middle of a water proof ground sheet. Buckets of water are placed behind it and small cups/beakers are scattered around. A poster reads: "Water – a Symbol of Life" and "The Spirit and the bride say, "Come." And let everyone who hears say, "Come." And let everyone who is thirsty come. Let anyone who wishes take the water of life as a gift. (Rev. 22:17). (If necessary facilitators can explain that the "bride" means the Church – the people of God.) Participants are invited to dip a cup into the bucket and pour it into the glass bowl. As they do so they pray for the people on their hearts, and also for themselves as they open themselves up to the Spirit's gift of life.

Lift Up Our Hearts!: A prayer for joy. Bottles of bubble fluid and wands are placed at this prayer station. As the bubbles rise and float so we ask God to lift our own hearts and the hearts of those for whom we are praying. A notice reads: "St. Paul writes: 'May you always be joyful in your union with the Lord, I say it again: rejoice! Show a gentle attitude towards everyone. The Lord is coming soon. Don't worry about anything but in all your prayers ask God for what you need, always asking him with a thankful heart. And God's peace, which is far beyond human understanding, will keep your hearts and minds in union with Christ Jesus'" (Philippians 4:4-7).[101]

In Christ God Emptied Himself for Us: A wooden cross is set up with a low candle in front of it. A notice reads: "Let the same mind be in you that was in Christ Jesus, who, though he was in the form of God, did not regard equality with God as something to be exploited, but emptied himself, taking the form of a slave, being born in human likeness. And being found in human form, he humbled himself and became obedient to the point of death — even death on a cross." (Philippians 2:4-8). Hard things happen to people. God is not someone who decided to stay away when things get tough. He helps those in the roughest situations. A box of stones is placed to one side and participants are invited to take one and place it at the foot of the cross. As they do so they bring the people whom they are thinking of – especially those in particular need – to God in prayer.

8. Half way through, the participants are asked to stop where they are and listen to a reading. This could be an appropriate bible reading or suitable poetry or prose depending on the make up of the participants.
9. When most people have completed a circuit of all the stations they are each given a votive candle. Those nearest to the low candles at the stations on each side of the church light their candles and pass on the light to the other participants. To the singing of "Who would true value see" or "I, the Lord of Sea and Sky" or "Brother, Sister let me serve you" or another suitable hymn, the participants move round the church in the same direction.
10. As the hymn comes to an end the people stop where they are and, facing inwards, join in with the prayer "Send us out into the world to live and serve you in the strength of your Holy Spirit. Amen." followed by the Lord's Prayer. The candles are extinguished and people hold hands for the Grace.
11. *Caring, Sharing* is played, then praise music as people leave. Each is given a bookmark with the words: "Living the Jesus Way" and information on future events.

Example 4. The Last Supper – Holy Communion

On arrival participants are greeted and invited to share in an informal gathering with refreshments. This is because we come to celebrate communion with one another in God. It is important to feel at ease with each other before we become quiet. In today's world, especially if we live in towns and cities but increasingly in the countryside too, we may not have spoken to the other people present for some days. Indeed there may very well be people who are strangers in church. These range from people on holiday to local people coming to church for the first time. It is difficult to under-estimate the cultural challenges of worship to people exploring faith, coming into a church where they have little contact with anyone before the service begins. Church-goers brought up in church ways may have been taught to keep complete silence prior to communion, and even to fast, as they prepare themselves for something very holy. There is much virtue in this and services should be available in which this practice is expected, but it is unrealistic and insensitive to force new people into this practice ten seconds after they have entered church.

Some lifelong church-goers are under the impression that Holy Communion is more difficult for newcomers than services of the word. This is not the case.

Since communion is rich with acted symbolism it is much easier for the uninitiated to grasp than much of the "church speak" that church-goers are used to. We use technical words (repentance, absolution, intercessions, salvation, collect, etc.) and short-cut expressions ("Jesus died for us", "born in the Spirit", etc.) which leave the uninitiated out in the cold. Sharing in Communion, sharing a symbolic meal, a meal in which Jesus is really present, is not only easier to understand it is also including and empowering. Very few newcomers are left unaware of the profound nature of the Holy Communion – yet it is less "frightening" for them than traditional church goers sometimes imagine.

Before the service Bread and Wine and Water are placed on a table in the centre of the nave. The bread should be a loaf and the wine should be in a wine bottle so that it is recognizable for what it is. The seats are placed around the nave in eleven groups each with a prominent notice displaying one of the names of the Twelve disciples, minus Judas. These could be banners that children or others have made prior to the worship. Providing a link with other activities (Sunday schools, home-groups etc.) is important. Worship leaders and facilitators are allocated to different groups. On one of the seats in each group is an envelop labelled "Invitation. Do not open yet!"" containing a piece of paper that says: "An invitation to the Lord's Supper. You are cordially invited to share in Jesus' love.", followed by the words of the response used at "7" below.

1. Participants are greeted on arrival and given an order of service and invited to share in the refreshments.
2. People are welcomed through the sound system and invited to find a seat anywhere around the church. Regular church goers should be aware of the need of families (especially newcomers) to sit together and ensure they do so.
3. The celebrant welcomes the people from in front of the altar.
4. The following verses are read from alongside the table on which stands the Bread and Wine:
5. "Jesus said to them, "I am the bread of life. Whoever comes to me will never be hungry, and whoever believes in me will never be thirsty.... Very truly, I tell you, whoever believes has eternal life. I am the bread of life. ... I am the living bread that came down from heaven. Whoever eats of this bread will live forever; and the bread that I will give for the life of the world is my flesh."" John 6:35, 47, 48 & 51
6. An appropriate hymn is sung such as "I am the Bread of Life". (*Mission Praise,* 80).[102]
7. The story of the origin of Holy Communion is explained by people in each group to their group, the events of the Last Supper being related in a way that

WELCOME TO St. WHATSIT'S, SOMEWHERE

The theme of our worship today is: **The Last Supper - Holy Communion**

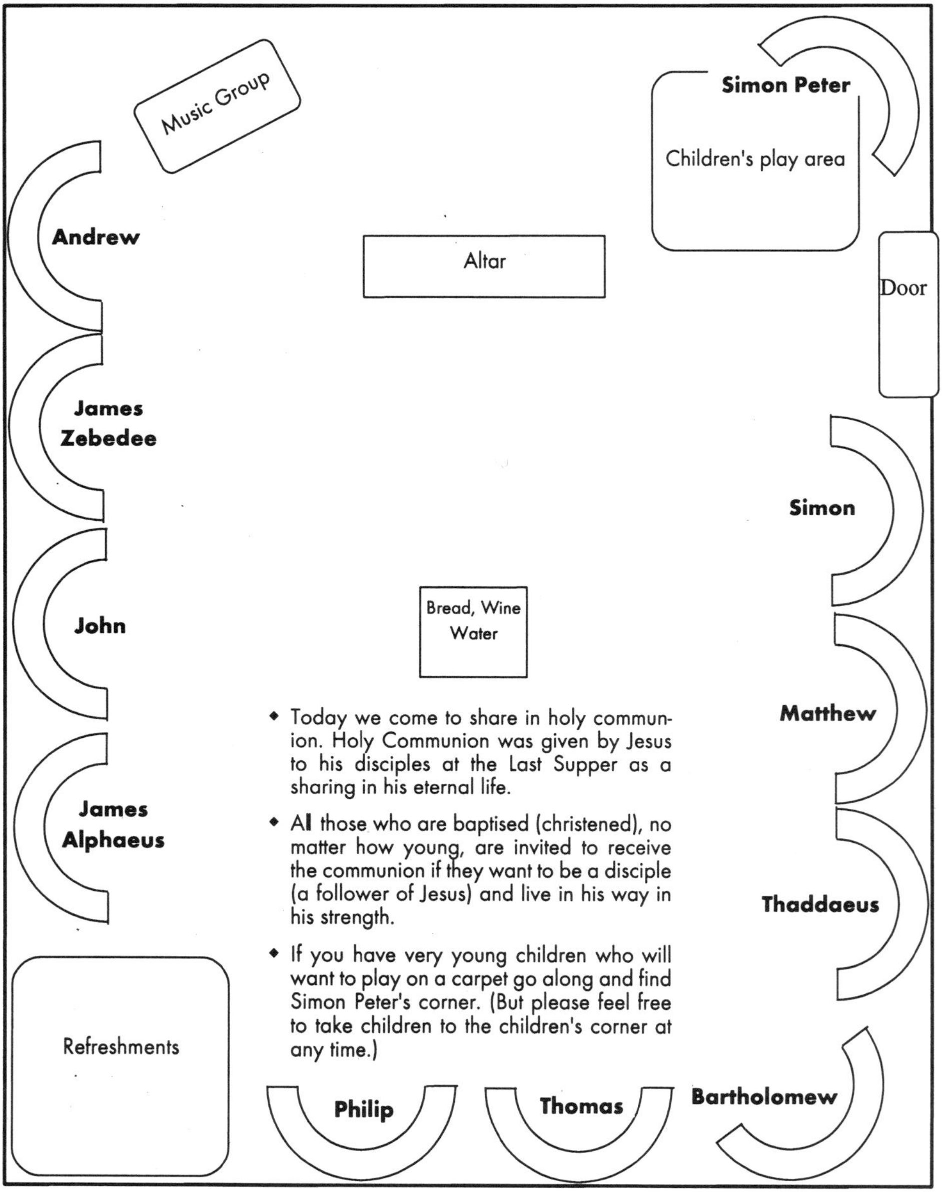

- Today we come to share in holy communion. Holy Communion was given by Jesus to his disciples at the Last Supper as a sharing in his eternal life.
- Al those who are baptised (christened), no matter how young, are invited to receive the communion if they want to be a disciple (a follower of Jesus) and live in his way in his strength.
- If you have very young children who will want to play on a carpet go along and find Simon Peter's corner. (But please feel free to take children to the children's corner at any time.)

PTO for the words of the hymns and prayers

members of the group can understand. Reference is made to the fact that we are all participants in the Lord's Supper too, and God knows each of us by name as much as he did those disciples at the first Lord's Supper.

8. Someone from each group takes the "invitation" envelope to another group and asks them to open it. The celebrant says: "Jesus is the Lamb of God who takes away the sins of the world. Blessed are those who are called to his supper. The participants respond (reading the invitation), "Lord, I am not worthy to receive you, but only say the word and I shall be healed.". A form of "Kyrie Confessions" is used (for example in *Common Worship*: 133). The celebrant pronounces an absolution.

9. An appropriate hymn is sung. If children or young people have prepared it before hand it is appropriate to come out and perform a "liturgical dance" around the table with the bread and wine on it. In some communities dance is especially appropriate and very well done. The dancers conclude by taking the bread, wine and water (and a "collection" if there is one) to the altar. Alternatively the bread and wine are brought by representatives of the participants. As it is received all join in saying a, "prayer at the preparation of the table" (*Common Worship*: 291).

10 A suitable Eucharistic Prayer is used (e.g. "Prayer D" or "H" from *Common Worship*), followed by silence and then the Lord's Prayer. The celebrant breaks the bread.

11. A form of the *Agnus Dei* is said or sung as the bread and wine is divided into eleven portions. Facilitators come forward from each of the eleven groups and the celebrant says: "God's holy gifts for God's holy people". The facilitators return with the bread which is shared among the people. They then do the same with the wine.

12. When all have communicated a suitable hymn is sung (e.g. "From hand to hand" (*Big Blue Planet:* 55))[103] and silence is kept.

13. A suitable post communion prayer is said and an affirmation followed by a post-communion hymn.

14. The worship concludes with a blessing and formal dismissal. The celebrant leaves and upbeat music is played and the people are free to interact informally.

NB. The pattern of this Holy Communion act of worship can be used around other themes. It does not always have to be on the theme of the Last Supper. It is a good idea, however, to do work on the story of the giving of Holy Communion fairly early on among those who are newcomers.

NOTES

1. See for example some of the stories on the Mothers' Union website: <www.themothersunion.org>.
2. In 2004 14,418 students sat A level Religious Studies in England and Wales. Almost three-quarters of these were girls. This was 1.9% of all students (2% sat French, 6.9% Maths and 10.7% English.). There were 12,671 in 2003, 10,685 in 2002 and 9532 in 2001. In 2004, among GCSE students, there were 141,037 entries in Religious Studies (2.4% of the total).
3. Danièle Hervieu-Léger (2000), *Religion as a Chain of Memory,* (Polity Press, Cambridge and Oxford).
4. Grace Davie (2000), *Religion in Modern Europe,* (OUP, Oxford) *et al.*
5. Introduced in the 1801 Concordat under Napoleon and formerly concluded in 1905 with the official law that separated Church from State, the concept of *laicité* is now embedded in French political culture. It ensures the liberty of conscience for each citizen. Each person can be religious, agnostic or an atheist according to preference without receiving special advantage or disadvantage. *Laicité* is particularly evident in state education where all forms of religious instruction or religious symbols or apparel are forbidden by law. *Laicité* should not be confused with secularism *per se* or anti-clericalism (as its name might suggest). See <www.laicite-laligue.org>
6. See the QCA website <www.qca.org.uk> for example. County agreed syllabi follow the same line.
7. *cf.* for example "The Beatitudes" (Matthew 5:1-12) and Jesus "first sermon" at Nazareth (Luke 4:16ff), *et al.*
8. William Caxton printed the first book in English in 1475 in Belgium and founded his press in London in the following year.
9. Ferdinand Megellan completed the first circumnavigation of the Earth in 1521.
10. The *Index of Forbidden Books* published by the Vatican. Anyone caught reading such books risked the penalty of excommunication (with the inevitable consequences that was believed to have for the after-life). The *Index* was finally abandoned in 1966. Copernicus' work was condemned by the Vatican in 1616.
11. After a lengthy trial lasting many years Galileo was eventually forced to "abjure" his belief in the Copernican system in 1633 and spent the rest of his life under house arrest. He was finally exonerated by the Catholic Church in 1992.
12. *Meditationes de Prima Philosophia* (1641).
13. The Council of Nicaea (325 CE).
14. Deism is the belief in one God who created in the beginning but who does not subsequently intervene in the universe. A kind of divine clock-maker who put the universe together, wound it up, and lets it run by itself.
15. Whilst Galileo's work was forbidden in his native Italy, for example, it was widely read and applauded in Protestant countries.
16. The term "Industrial Revolution" was first used in the early 19th century.
17. South American "Liberation Theology", as it was to become known, was developed in the works of Ruben Alves and Gustavo Gutierrez and later Leonardo Boff and others in the late 1960s and 1970s.
18. David Sheppard's *Built as a City* (1974) and *Bias to the Poor* (1983) (both Hodder and Stoughton) were important precursors to the Church of England report *Faith in the City* (1986). See also Schottroff and Stegemann, *Jesus and the Hope of the Poor* (1978) (Orbis Books).

19. see Carpenter, 16.
20. A subsequently repentant college was to found an F. D. Maurice Chair of Moral Theology.
21. Chris.Livesey: <www.sociology.org.uk> Pg 2.
22. Herbert Spencer and W. E. H. Lecky for example. For Spencer (writing in 1892), "man was a product of the evolutionary process, and, in the absence of any transcendental source of moral values, he would have to create a new ethics based on the guidance of nature itself" (Bowler, 207).
23. *cf.* Kenneth Leech, (1973) *Youthquake : the growth of a counter-culture through two decades.* (London : Sheldon Press).
24. For example Pauline studies prior to E. P. Sanders who revolutionised the thinking in the middle 1970s. *cf.* E. P. Sanders (1977) *Paul and Palestinian Judaism : a comparison of patterns of religion.* (SCM, London).
25. The famous *Droits de l'Homme"* of the French Revolution.
26. See <www.swif.it/foldop/>
27. See <http://en.wikipedia.org/wiki/Grand_unification_theory> for a summary of the current models.
28. See <http://p076.ezboard.com/frealismfreeforall.showMessage?topic ID=997.topic>
29. Witton, *Universe on a String <http://www.sns.ias.edu/~witten/>*. See also Barton Zwiebach (2004), *A First Course in String Theory* (Cambridge University Press).
30. Rodney Dennis Holder (2005), *God the Multiverse and Everything: Modern Cosmology and the Argument from Design* (Ashgate).
31. James Lovelock (2000): *Gaia: A New Look at Life on Earth* (Oxford Paperbacks).
32. <www.gaianet.fsbusiness.co.uk/gaiatheory.html>
33. In recent years campaigns organized by Christian Aid, the World Development Movement and the Fair Trade companies themselves have seen the introduction of Fair Trade goods on supermarket shelves. The Co-operative outlets have taken the lead in this.
34. For example, The "Living Churchyard" competitions of recent years. See also: Cooper, Nigel, (1995) *Wildlife in Church & Churchyard.* (Church House Publishing),
35. *cf.* Michael Mitton (1995) *Restoring the Woven Cord: Principles of Celtic Christianity for the Church Today* (Darton, Longman & Todd Ltd).
36. Julian L. Simon, "What Does the Future Hold" in Julian L. Simon (1995) *The State of Humanity* (Oxford, UK : Blackwell in association with the Cato Institute).
37. Institut Agricole de l'abbaye Montebourg.
38. Allan Bloom – an American political theorist who died in 1992.
39. Computing has promoted this type of thought. The use of "hypertext" (a term first coined by Ted Nelson in 1965) and more recently "hypermedia" to access information in a non-linear way has freed people from dependence on linear forms of communication such as speech, books and film. It has not only transformed study technique and access to information through the World Wide Web, it has also influenced the arts, with films such as Quentin Tarrantino's *Pulp Fiction* (1994) for example. Human thought, based as it is on neural networks, is fundamentally non-linear.
40. The Uncertainty Principle concerns the inability of investigators to determine both the position and momentum of a given particle. As soon as you attempt to measure a particle it alters its momentum.
41. Particle-Wave duality applies to light which can behave both as waves and particles (photons). Similarly electrons can sometimes act like waves rather than particles. This relates to the uncertainty principle since entities that are both waves and particles can never be held to be in a particular place or travelling in a particular direction at any given time.

42. *cf.* Adrian Thatcher (1999) *Marriage after Modernity: Christian Marriage in Postmodern Times* (Sheffield academic Press, Sheffield).

43. "Glass ceiling" refers to the ability of women to rise to a certain level in institutions and progress no further. Men generally seem to procure the really top jobs. See for example : Carole Kadinger Adair (1999) *Cracking the Glass Ceiling: Factors Influencing Women's Attainment of Senior Executive Positions.* In the Church of England the ceiling is not "glass" because women are simply not permitted to be consecrated bishops.

44. Urban Priority Areas' areas are determined by indicators or deprivation – unemployment, old people living alone, single-parent families, ethnicity, overcrowding of homes and homes lacking basic amenities. (Faith in the City, 10).

45. Since 1948, the Annie E. Casey Foundation (AECF) has worked to build better futures for disadvantaged children and their families in the United States. The primary mission of the Foundation is to foster public policies, human service reforms, and community supports that more effectively meet the needs of today's vulnerable children and families. See <www.aecf.org>.

46. Defined as, "British slang for a swaggering, drunken, uncouth young woman" by the Probert Encyclopaedia: Slang (L-Ld) <www.probertencyclopaedia.com/ZL.HTM>

47. Play is essential for all generations, not just children.

48. The current Anti-social Behaviour Act 2003 (section 30) allows the police to disperse any group if they believe (a) that any members of the public have been intimidated, harassed, alarmed or distressed as a result of the presence or behaviour of groups of two or more persons in public places in any locality in his police area (the "relevant locality"), and (b) that anti-social behaviour is a significant and persistent problem in the relevant locality. They can take home any individual aged under the age 16 meeting with one or more others between the hours of 9 pm. and 6 am. who does not appear to be under the supervision of someone aged 18 over.

49. In my experience in parish ministry, the breakdown of family life comes second only to the death of a parent in disrupting a young person's confidence or well-being. Depending on the nature of the rupture a death may even be less harmful. A dysfunctional family is nearly always better than a broken one.

50. For example, *Al-Qaeda* means "The Network".

51. From the hymn "There is a Green Hill Far Away" by Cecil Frances Alexander (1818-1895).

52. Quantum physics thinks in terms of the universe as a combination of particles, events and relationships. The universe can thus be described as created in the image of God in this sense.

53. The doctrine that it is possible only to say what God is not.

54. ed. W. H. Gardener (1953), *Gerard Manly Hopkins: A Selection of his Poetry and Prose,* (The Penguin Poets). See also <http://www.poetsgraves.co.uk/Classic%20Poems/Hopkins/god's_grandeur.htm>.

55. See, for example, Steven Bouma-Prediger (1995) *The Greening of Theology: The Ecological Models of Rosemary Radford Ruether, Joseph Sittler, and Jurgen Moltmann* (American Academy of Religion Academy, No 91) and Sean McDonagh (1990) *The Greening of the Church,* (Orbis Books – USA) and Sean McDonagh (1986) *To Care for the Earth: a Call to a New Theology* (Cassel – London).

56. The Salvation Army was founded in 1865 in London by the English Methodist minister William Booth.

57. Founded in 1882, the (Anglican) Church Army was the idea of another London cleric, Wilson Carlile.

58. "Church of England Central Home for Waifs and Strays" was the idea of Edward Rudolf in 1881. The first home was in Dulwich, London (1882).

59. See <http://www.the-childrens-society.org.uk/learn/SG_Feature/5926/2/>

60. Note; The Guardian's obituary on Lord Runcie (Archbishop of Canterbury at the time) by Stephen Bates, Thursday July 13, 2000.

61. See <http://www.christianaid.org.uk/caweek03/what_we_do/what_we_believe.php>

62. See QCA Religious studies for GCSE, for example.

63. From "Death is Nothing at All" by Henry Scott Holland (1847-1918).

64. Arranged by W. G. Hathaway (1935) Moody Bible Institute of Chicago.

65. *Common Worship, Services and Prayers for the Church of England* (2000) (Church House Publishing) Pg. 355.

66. The *Alpha Course* emanates from Holy Trinity Brompton, London (see <http://alphacourse.org>) and the *Emmaus Course* and related resources are produced by the National Society (see <http://www.natsoc.org.uk/emmaus/>). *Emmaus* is less of a package than *Alpha* being designed to be adaptable and a set of resources. Nevertheless it remains a "course".

67. In one place I came across quite a phalanx of child servers and choir members with a very good record of attendance. After a short time I discovered they were each given between £2 and £5 per service attended. Counting numbers under these circumstances would appear misleading.

68. Reading the history of the prebendary stalls of Salisbury Cathedral, for example, is quite depressing. See Christopher Ross (2000), *Canons of Salisbury: A Record of the Dignitaries, Prebendaries and Office Holders and Their Place in the Quire of Salisbury Cathedral* (Salisbury Cathedral).

69. *cf.* Matthew 25:31-46.

70. See, for example, Edward J. Larson (2002), *Trial and Error: The American Controversy Over Creation and Evolution* (OUP in the USA).

71. See ed. R.Scott Appleby, Martin E. Marty (1995) five volumes on the *The Fundamentalism Project* (University of Chicago Press) and Karen Armstrong (2001), *The Battle for God: Fundamentalism in Judaism, Christianity and Islam,* (Harper Collins, London) *et al.*

72. See <www.sspx.org>.

73. ibid.

74. ed. R.Scott Appleby, Martin E. Marty (1995) five volumes on the *The Fundamentalism Project* (University of Chicago Press).

75. ACRE, Somerford Court, Somerford Road, Cirencester, Gloucestershire GL7 1TW. See <www.acre.org.uk>

76. Campaign to Protect Rural England, 128 Southwark Street, London, SE1 0SW. See <www.cpre.org.uk>

77. "Farm Crisis Network" A partnership between the Arthur Rank Centre and the Agricultural Christian Fellowship.

78. This changed with recommendations in *Faith in the Countryside* (1991). From 2004 the Disability Discrimination Act requires the church to take notice of the needs of those with disabilities. The State can appear more aware than the Church in some areas.

79. *"croyants baladeurs"*. A *baladeur* can also mean a personal audio-device – a "walkman" or an "ipod".

80. Danièle Hervieu-Léger (1999), *Le Pèlerin et le Converti: la religion en mouvement,* (Flammarion – Paris).

81. Thornton, L.S (1952) *The Dominion of Christ,* (Dacre Press, London).

82. Cupitt, Don. (1984) *The Sea of Faith* (British Broadcasting Corporation, London).

83. <www.sofn.org.uk>.

84. See <salisbury.anglican.org/support/pdev/bcce.htm>.

85. See <www.ex.ac.uk/theology/ug/cert/f2f.html> at Exeter University.

86. See <www.sarum.ac.uk> at Sarum College.

87. See, for example, Ian Tarrant and Sally Dakin (2004) *Labyrinths and Prayer Stations* (Grove Booklets W180, Cambridge).

88. Some churches even have refreshments in the middle of the worship.

89. In the Church of England these are called canons. See <www.cofe.anglican.org/legal/canons.html>.

90. The Anglican Bridport Team Ministry, Dorset.

91. It is important that each church should have a child protection policy with guidelines for safe practice. See *Protecting all God's Children: The Child Protection Policy for the Church of England, 3rd edition,* Church House Publishing (2004), for example.

92. The Church Urban Fund, launched in the wake of *Faith in the City* (1986) supports projects in the poorest parts of England. <http://www.cuf.org.uk/>

93. Lee Abbey Christian Community, Devon <http://www.leeabbey.org.uk/>

94. Philip Pullman's trilogy was written between 1995 and 2000. Aimed at the teenage market, it has become popular among adults too. Published by Scholastic Children's Books the three titles are *Northern Lights, The Subtle Knife* and *The Amber Spyglass.*

95. *The Bridport News,* September 1996.

96. For those who are interested, one way to answer the question "Who made God?" that children often ask is get them to see that they are making assumptions about God that only apply to creation. For example, ask the child, "If I told you Izzy-Whizzy made God, what would your next question be?". When they reply "Who made Izzy-Whizzy?" (which they always do) I reply, "Umbly-Jumbly". Even 9 years olds can see it has to stop somewhere... . Then I ask, "Why does God have to have been made? Sure, everything we know in the world has had a beginning, but why does God have to have had one? Part of being God is that always was, is, and will be for ever." Children accept that. The answer is honest, but not dismissive. After one challenging question, I recall one adult interjecting, "Don't ask the minister that. It's rude!". Whatever the intention of the questioner, questions about the nature of God or faith are nearly always valid.

97. Clergy can given countless examples. "She never went to church again after X told her her singing was terrible.", claimed one family when we were preparing an old lady's funeral, "None of us have had anything to do with God since!". I met X. The damage she had done was enormous – but in her arrogance she never admitted it.

98. Salisbury Diocesan order for the licensing of a new priest.

99. More information about labyrinths can be found at <www.lessons4living.com/labyrinth.htm>.

100. By Linda Caroe. *Big Blue Planet,* ed Judy Jarvis (1995), (Stainer and Bell & the Methodist Church Division of Education and Youth, UK).

101. from the Good News Bible.

102. Written by Suzann Toolan. *Mission Praise,* ed. Fudge, Horrobin & Leavers (1967), (Marshall, Morgan and Scott).

103. By Andrew Eaton. *Big Blue Planet,* ed Judy Jarvis (1995), (Stainer and Bell & the Methodist Church Division of Education and Youth, UK).

Bibliography

ARMSTRONG, Karen, (2000), *The Battle for God : Fundamentalism in Judaism, Christianity and Islam,* (London : Harper Collins).

ATHERTON, John, (1992), *Christianity and the Market: Christian Social Thought for our Times,* (London : SPCK).

BAKER, Jonny and GAY, Doug, (2003), *Alternative Worship,* (London : SPCK).

BARRETT, Michèle & PHILLIPS, Anne, (1992) *Destabilizing Theory : Contemporary Feminist Debates,* (Cambridge : Polity Press).

BAUDRILLARD, Jean, (1994) *The Illusion of the End,* (Cambridge : Polity Press).

BAUDRILLARD, Jean, (1988) *Selected Writings,* Edited by Mark Poster, (Cambridge : Polity Press).

BAUMAN, Zygmunt, (2000), *Liquid Modernity* (Cambridge : Polity Press).

BOSCOVICH, Ruggiero Giuseppe, (1763), *A theory of natural philosophy put forward and explained by Roger Joseph Boscovich* ; English edition [translated by J. M. Child] from the text of the first Venetian edition published in 1763. With a short life of Boscovich [by Branislav Petronievic. First published with the Latin text by Open Court Publishing Company in 1922]. (Cambridge, Mass : MIT Press, 1966).

BOWLER, PETER J. (1990), *Charles Darwin – The Man and his Influence* (Cambridge, Massachusetts : Basil Blackwell, Inc.).

BRANNEN, Julia, DODD, Kathryn, OAKLEY, Ann, STOREY, Pamela, (1994), *Young People, Health and Family Life,* (Buckingham : Open University Press).

BRICO, Rex, (1978), *Taizé: Brother Roger and his Community,* (London; Glasgow : Collins).

BROWN, Callum G. (2001), *The Death of Christian Britain,* (London : Routledge).

CARPENTER, Spencer Cecil, (1959), *Church and People, 1789-1889 : a history of the Church of England.* (London : S.P.C.K.).

CUPITT, Don. (1984) *The Sea of Faith* (London : British Broadcasting Corporation).

DAMRELL, Joseph, (1978), *Search for Identity : Youth, Religion, and Culture,* (Beverly Hills, California; London : Sage Publications).

DAVIE, Grace, (2000), *Religion in Modern Europe : a Memory Mutates,* (Oxford University Press).

DAVIE, Grace, (2002), *Europe : the Exceptional Case : parameters of faith in the modern world,* (Darton, Longman and Todd).

DODD, C. H. (Charles Harold), (1936), *The Apostolic Preaching and its Developments,* (London : Hodder).

ELLUL, Jacques, (1973), *Propaganda: The Formation of Men's Attitudes,* (New York : 1973).

ELLUL, Jacques, (1984), *La Subversion du Christianisme,* (Paris : La Table Ronde).

FIDDES, Paul S., (2000), *Participating in God : a Pastoral Doctrine of the Trinity,* (London : Darton Longman & Todd).

GONZALES-BALADO, J. L. (2003), *The Story of Taizé,* (London : Continuum).

GRAHAM, Elaine, (1996), *Transforming Practice: Pastoral Theology in an Age of Uncertainty,* (London : Mowbray).

HANDY, Charles B., (1994), *The Age of Paradox,* (Boston, Mass. : Harvard Business School Press).

HANSON, R. P. C., (1967), *The Acts in the Revised Standard Version: with introduction and commentary,* (Oxford: Clarendon Press).

HEAVEN, Patrick C. L., (1996), *Adolescent Health : the Role of Individual Differences,* (London : Routledge).

HEBERT Gabriel (1956), *Fundamentalism of the Church of God* (London : SCM).

HERVIEU-LÉGER, Danièle, (1999), *La Religion en Mouvement : le pèlerin et le converti* (Paris : Flammarion).

HERVIEU-LÉGER, Danièle, (2000), *Religion as a Chain of Memory* (London : Polity Press).

HIMMELFARB, Gertrude, (1995), *The De-moralization of Society: from Victorian virtues to modern values,* (London : Institute of Economic Affairs Health & Welfare Unit).

JACKSON, Bob, (2002) *Hope for the Church: Contemporary Strategies for Growth,* (London : Church House Publishing).

JOHN, Brother of Taizé, (1995), *God of the Unexpected,* (London : Geoffrey Chapman Mowbray).

KÜNG Hans & MOLTMANN Jürgen eds. (1992) *Fundamentalism as an Ecumenical Challenge,* pp. 80-88 (HEBBLETHWAITE Peter, *A Fundamentalist Pope?*) and pp. 106-116 (KÜNG Hans *Against Contemporary Roman Catholic Fundamentalism*), (London : SCM Press).

KÜNG Hans, (1971), *Infallible – An Enquiry,* (London : SCM Press).

KÜNG Hans, (1963), *The Living Church: Reflections on the Second Vatican Council,* (London & New York : Sheed & Ward).

KÜNG Hans, (1977), *On Being a Christian,* (London : Collins).

KÜNG Hans, (1995), *Christianity: The Religious Situation of Our Time,* (London : SCM).

LEECH, Kenneth, (1973), *Youthquake: the growth of a counter-culture through two decades,* (London : Sheldon Press).

LOVELOCK, James, (2000), *Gaia : a New Look at Life on Earth,* (Oxford : Oxford University Press).

McROBBIE, Angela, (2000), *Feminism and Youth Culture,* (Basingstoke : Macmillan).

MARTY, Martin E. and APPLEBY, R. Scott. (1991) *Fundamentalisms Observed: a Study Conducted by the American Academy of Arts and* Sciences, (Chicago ; London : University of Chicago Press).

MITTON, Michael, (1995), *Restoring the Woven Cord: Strands of Celtic Christianity for the Church Today,* (London : Darton, Longman and Todd).

MOORE, James R. (1979), *The Post Darwinian Controversies – A Study of the Protestant Struggle to Come to Terms with Darwin in Great Britain and America 1870 – 1900* (Cambridge University Press).

RIDDELL, Michael, (1998), *Threshold of the Future: Reforming the Church in the Post-Christian West,* (London : SPCK).

ROBINSON, John A. T. (John Arthur Thomas) (1963), *Honest to God,* (London : SCM).

ROGERS, Chris, (2004), *Naked Christianity,* (Kevin Mayhew, Stowmarket, Suffolk, England).

SCHILLEBEECKX, Edward, (1980), *Christ: the Christian Experience in the Modern World,* (London : SCM Press Ltd.).

SCHILLEBEECKX, Edward, (1990), *Church : the Human Story of God,* (London: SCM Press).

SCHOTTROFF and STEGEMANN, (1978), *Jesus and the Hope of the Poor* (New York : Orbis Books).

SHEPPARD, David, (1974), *Built as a City : God and the urban world today,* (London : Hodder and Stoughton).

SHEPPARD, David, (1983), *Bias to the Poor,* (London : Hodder and Stoughton).

SIMON, Julian (1995), *The State of Humanity,* (Oxford : Blackwell in association with the Cato Institute).

STERNHEIMER, Karen. (2003), *It's Not the Media : The Truth about Pop Culture's Influence on Children,* (Boulder, Colo. ; Oxford : Westview).

TARRANT, Ian and DAKIN, Sally (2004), *Labyrinths and Prayer Stations,* (Cambridge : Grove Booklets Worship Series).

THATCHER, Adrian, (1999), *Marriage after Modernity: Christian Marriage in Postmodern Times,* (Sheffield : Sheffield Academic Press).

WARD, Pete, (2002), *Liquid Church,* (Carlisle, Cumbria, UK : Paternoster Press).

WRIGHT, Michael, (1975), *New Ways for Christ,* (London & Oxford : Mowbray).

WOODS, Tim, (1999), *Beginning Postmodernism,* (Manchester : Manchester University Press).

ZOHAR, Danah, (1991), *The Quantum Self*, (London : Flamingo).

CHURCH PUBLICATIONS

Board of Education of the General Synod of the Church of England, (1996), *Tomorrow is Another Country: Education in a Post-Modern World,* (London : Church House Publishing).

Church of England's Mission and Public Affairs Council, (2004), *Mission-Shaped Church: Church Planting and Special Expressions of Church in a Changing Context,* (London : Church House Publishing).

House of Bishops of the General Synod of the Church of England, (2004), *Protecting All God's Children: The Child Protection Policy for the Church of England, 3rd Edition,* (London : Church House Publishing).

Mission Theological Advisory Group, (2002), *Presence and Prophecy: A Heart for Mission in Theological Education,* (London : Churches Together in Britain and Ireland and Church House Publishing).

Report of the Archbishop of Canterbury's Commission on Urban Priority Areas, (1985), *Faith in the City: A Call for Action by Church and Nation,* (London : Church House Publishing).

Report of the Archbishops' Commission on Rural Areas, (1990), *Faith in the Countryside,* (Worthing, West Sussex : Churchman Publishing).

Report of the Review of the Dioceses, Pastoral and related Measures, (2004), *A Measure for Measures: In mission and ministry,* (London : Church House Publishing).